SCHOLASTIC COLLECTIONS
Compiled by Jill Bennett

Early Years
Poems & Rhymes

© 1993 Scholastic Ltd
5 6 7 8 9   8 9 0 1 2

Published by Scholastic Ltd,
Villiers House,
Clarendon Avenue,
Leamington Spa,
Warwickshire CV32 5PR

Compiler Jill Bennett
Editor Jane Wright
Series designer Joy White
Cover and illustrations Valeria Petrone

Designed using Aldus Pagemaker
Artwork by David Harban Design, Warwick

British Library Cataloguing-in-Publication Data
A catalogue record for this book is
available from the British Library.

ISBN 0-590-53053-4

Contents

ALL SORTS OF PEOPLE

PLAYTIME

Acknowledgements

**The publishers gratefully acknowledge permission
to reproduce the following copyright material:**

© 1991 Abecedarius Books for 'A piece of sun', trans by Philip de Vos from *My Drum 2*; A & C Black for 'Tree' © 1991 Jenny Boult from *The Green Umbrella*, 'Windscreen wiper' © 1964 S K Vickery from *Rhythm Rhymes*; Angus & Robertson for 'Scooter' © 1987 Lydia Pender from *Morning Magpie*; BBC Publications for 'Counting' and 'One pink sari' © 1992 Ann Marie Linden from *Steel Drums*; Bell & Hyman for 'Yellow' © 1984 Olive Dove from *Sit on the Roof and Holler*; © 1993 Colin Bennett for 'Pupa'; © 1993 Jill Bennett for 'Diwali morning' and 'Packed lunch'; Blackie & Sons for 'Water everywhere' © 1991 Valerie Bloom from *Can I Buy a Slice of Sky?*, 'The hat of the house' © 1991 Stanley Cook from *The Poem Box*, 'Hair-drier' © 1989 Maggie Holmes from *Things That Go*; The Bodley Head for 'Lollipop lady' © 1983 John Agard from *I din' do nuttin*, 'Foot marching', 'Polishing Grandad' and 'Driving Grandad' © 1992 Jean Willis from *Toffee Pockets*; © 1993 Ann Bonner for 'Friend', 'Getting dressed' and 'Happy Diwali'; © 1993 Tony Bradman for 'My telescope' and 'Potty but true'; CEM for 'Someone' by Susan Schutz from *Exploring a Theme: Me and My Community* ; © 1993 Sue Cowling for 'Come October', 'Islands' and 'Where?'; © Niru Desai for 'Ek ne ek be' from *Sing Along*;; © 1993 Gina Douthwaite for 'Knickers', 'Lazy day' and 'Road sweeper machine'; © 1993 Eleanor Farjeon for 'New clothes and old'; © 1993 John Foster for 'Christmas wishes', 'It's Pancake Day', 'My old blue shirt', 'Shoes', 'Ted', 'Ten white snowmen', 'The double-decker bus', 'There's a hole in my pants', 'This morning my dad shouted' and 'When Susie eats custard'; © 1993 Janet Greenyer for 'Guy Fawkes Night' and 'The festival of Holi'; © 1993 Romesh Gunesekera for 'Kandy Blue and Balaballoo'; © 1993 Theresa Heine for 'Bag of mixed candy', 'Balloon seller', 'Christmas counting', 'Seasons turn', 'Spring sunshine', 'Vanessa or the lucky egg' and 'Weather'; Heinemann Educational for 'Winter' and 'A lucky bag dip' © 1979 Cynthia Mitchell from *Hop along happily*; Heinemann Young Books for 'Food' (1987) and 'Take two cushions' (1984) © Tony Bradman from *A Kiss on the Nose*; Hutchinson Publishing Group Ltd for 'I know a little house' © 1984 Valerie McCarthy from *Nursery Rhymes and Songs from Listen with Mother*; © Barbara Ireson for 'Aeroplanes, aeroplanes' (1978), 'All alone' (1978), 'In Regents Park' (1993) and 'Pussy walks softly' (1993); Islamic Foundation for 'Bread Man! Bread Man!' and 'Little pony' from *Muslim Nursery Rhymes*; Julia MacRae for 'I live in a hut' and 'Eating an icicle' © 1981 Nancy Chambers from *Stir-about*; © 1993 Jean Kenward for 'Apple crumble', 'Bobble', 'Ducks feeding', 'Gulls', 'Homes', 'Hunting song', 'Jumping song', 'Letters', 'Little Miss Pidget', 'Mouse', 'Nothing', 'Ogre', 'Rain and snow', 'Some people', 'Star song', 'The paint box', 'Transport' and 'Wind'; © 1993 Ian Larmont for 'Fastening buttons', 'Happy Christmas', 'Owl' and 'Tea time'; © Wendy Larmont for 'Eid' (1993), 'November the Fifth' (1993), 'Reflections' (1991) and 'Winter walk' (1993); Lutterworth Press for 'Badgers' and 'How?' © 1986 Richard Edwards from *The Word Party*; © 1993 Beverley McLoughland for 'Annie, Annie' and 'Secret'; Macmillan Caribbean for 'Let's talk' © Telcine Turner; © 1993 Wes Magee for 'Christmas travellers', 'Inside your house', 'I want....', 'So you want to be a wizard' and 'Three taps'; © 1993 Robin Mellor for 'Froggles', 'My teddy bear' and 'Tea trouble'; Methuen Children's Books for 'The puffin' and 'The jigsaw bird' © 1989 Mark Burgess from *Feeling Beastly*, 'What are friends like?' © 1982 Ruth Kirtley from *Seeing and Doing*, 'Comforting thought' © 1990 Hiawyn Oram from *Speaking for Ourselves* and 'Don't jump in puddles' and 'Who did it?' by Irene Rawnsley from *Dog's Dinner*; © 1993 Tony Mitton for 'Hairwashing', 'Jam', 'Rain rhymes', 'Sea song', 'Storm', 'Sympathy', 'Ten for the day', 'The soap fish', 'The Underground Snake', 'Towers', 'What is under?' and 'Who's there?'; © 1993 Brian Moses for 'Goodnight' and 'To the fair'; Multicultural Service (Wolverhampton) for 'Rayri wallah geet' from *Songs for a Multicultural School*; © 1993 Judith Nicholls for 'Fireworks!', 'Giant's breakfast', 'Help, it's raining!', 'Humpty Dumpty's fruit pie', 'Id-al-fitr', 'Strawberry pie', 'There's a spider in my bath!', 'Train ride', 'Who?' and 'Winter morning'; Oxford University Press for 'Immediate dispatch' © 1980 Jean Gilbert from *Topic Anthology*, 'The little red bus' © 1980 Michael John from *Topic Anthology*, 'Night rider' © 1980 Margaret McCarthy, 'Living-places' © 1980 Julie Norman and 'Chinese New Year' © 1980 Dorothy Richards from *Big Dipper*; © 1993 Isobel Pratt for 'Safety yellow'; © 1993 Janis Priestley for 'Granny's alarm'; © Irene Rawnsley for 'Bobby Bottle Mouse' (1993); © Michael Rosen for 'Here comes the robot', 'Humpty Dumpty went to the moon', 'I don't like custard' (1990) and 'Stamp, stamp, stamp' (1985); © 1991 Vyanne Samuels for 'Peace'; Scholastic Children's Books Ltd for 'Playtime' © 1990 Penelope Browning from *Crocodile Tears*; © 1993 Ian Souter for 'Inside my own house', 'Jelly wobbles', 'Me!', 'My Aunty Maisie', 'Today for lunch!' and 'Together, whatever the weather'; © 1993 Charles Thomson for 'Looping the loop', 'New clothes', 'New wheelchair', 'People in the house', 'Sally' and 'This old house'; Transworld Publishing Ltd for 'Granny Brigg's baking day' and 'The Seashell' © l980 Daphne Lister from *Gingerbread Pigs*; Viking Children's Books for 'Can I come along?' and 'Kiss me quickly' © Tony Bradman from *All Together Now*, 'High on the wall' © 1986 Charles Causley from *Early in the Morning*, 'Winter parcel' © 1991 Linda Hammond from *One Blue Boat* and 'In case you didn't know' and 'Night lights' © 1989 Michelle Magorian from *Waiting for My Shorts to Dry*; Walker Books for 'Feasts', 'Fire', 'Seaside', 'Sick', 'Squirting rainbows' and 'Sunshine' © 1988 Shirley Hughes from *Out and About*; © 1993 Colin West for 'Uncle Paul'; © l984 Gordon Winch for 'The telly monster'; © l99l Irene Yates for 'Journey into space'.

Every effort has been made to trace copyright holders for the poems in this anthology and the publishers apologise for an inadvertent omissions.

ANIMALS

The little black dog

The little black dog ran round the house,
And set the bull a-roaring,
And drove the monkey in the boat,
Who set the oars a-rowing,
And scared the cock upon the rock,
Who cracked his throat with crowing.

Anonymous

Cock and hen

Cock: Lock the dairy door,
Lock the dairy door!
Hen: Chickle, chackle, chee,
I haven't got the key.

Anonymous

Goose feathers

Cackle, cackle, Mother Goose,
Have you any feathers loose?
Truly have I, pretty fellow,
Half enough to fill a pillow.
Here are quills, take one or two,
And down to make a bed for you.

Anonymous

The flying pig

Dickery, dickery dare,
The pig flew up in the air;
The man in brown
Soon brought him down,
Dickery, dickery, dare.

Anonymous

Little Blue Ben

Little Blue Ben, who lives in the glen,
Keeps a blue cat and one blue hen,
Which lays of blue eggs a score and ten;
Where shall I find the little Blue Ben?

Anonymous

The donkey

If I had a donkey that wouldn't go,
Would I beat him? Oh no, no.
I'd put him in the barn and give him some corn,
The best little donkey that ever was born.

Anonymous

The old grey donkey

Donkey, donkey, old and grey,
Open your mouth and gently bray;
Lift your ears and blow your horn,
To wake the world this sleepy morn.

Anonymous

Dame Trot

Dame Trot and her cat
Sat down for a chat;
The dame sat on this side
And puss sat on that.

Puss, says the Dame,
Can you catch a rat,
Or a mouse in the dark?
Purr, says the cat.

Anonymous

Bagpipes

Puss came dancing out of a barn
With a pair of bagpipes under her arm;
She could sing nothing but Fiddle-cum-fee,
The mouse has married the humble-bee.
Pipe, cat – dance, mouse –
We'll have a wedding at our good house.

Anonymous

Pussy in de moonlight

Pussy in de moonlight
Pussy in de zoo
Pussy never come home
Till half past two.

traditional Caribbean

Hoddley poddley

Hoddley, poddley, puddle and frogs,
Cats are to marry the poodle dogs;
Cats in blue jackets and dogs in red hats,
What will become of the mice and the rats?

Anonymous

Six little mice

Six little mice sat down to spin;
Pussy passed by and she peeped in.
What are you doing, my little men?
Weaving coats for gentlemen.
Shall I come in and cut off your threads?
No, no, Mistress Pussy, you'd bite off our heads.
Oh, no, I'll not; I'll help you to spin.
That may be so, but you don't come in.

Anonymous

Pussycat Mole

Pussycat Mole jumped over a coal
And in her best petticoat burnt a great hole.
Poor Pussy's weeping, she'll have no more milk
Until her best petticoat's mended with silk.

Anonymous

There was a little boy

There was a little boy went into a barn,
And lay down on some hay;
An owl came out and flew about,
And the little boy ran away.

Anonymous

Down on the farm

The cock's on the woodpile
Blowing his horn,
The bull's in the barn
A-threshing the corn,
The maids in the meadow
Are making the hay,
The ducks in the river
Are swimming away.

Anonymous

Me cock a crow

Me cock a crow –
coo-coo-ri-co,
before day him a crow –
coo-coo-ri-coo,
him a crow fe me wake –
coo-coo-ri-coo.

traditional Jamaican

This little pig

This little pig had a rub-a-dub,
This little pig had a scrub-a-scrub,
This little pig-a-wig ran upstairs,
This little pig-a-wig called out, Bears!
Down came the jar with a loud Slam! Slam!
And this little pig had all the jam.

Anonymous

Jack Sprat's pig

Little Jack Sprat
Once had a pig;
It was not very little,
And not very big,
It was not very lean,
It was not very fat –
'It's a good pig to grunt,'
Said Little Jack Sprat.

Anonymous

Here is the ostrich

Here is the ostrich, straight and tall,
(Raise arm, fingers drooping.)
Nodding his head above us all.

Here is the long snake on the ground,
(Wiggle hand and arm.)
Wriggling on the stones he found.

Here are the birds that fly so high,
(Flap arms.)
Spreading their wings across the sky.

Here is the hedgehog, prickly and small,
(Clench fist.)
Rolling himself into a ball.

Here is the spider scuttling round,
(Walk fingers like spider.)
Treading so lightly on the ground.

Here are the children fast asleep,
(Rest head on hands clasped palm to palm.)
And here at night the owls do peep.
*(Make thumb and fingers into spectacles
around eyes, move head side to side.)*

Anonymous

Madari

Bandar ne pyjama pahena
Bandhariya ne kapada gahena
Khoob madari eneh nachata
Damroo baja bajakar gata.
traditional Hindi

Monkey is wearing pyjamas,
She monkey some jewellery and clothes.
The performing monkey man makes them dance
As he sings and plays his little drum.

Cuckadoo-cu

Apne kalangi uche karke
Murga bola cuckadoo-cu
Huaa savera jago bhai
Cuckadoo-cu bhai cuckadoo-cu
traditional Hindi

Raising his head,
The cock says, 'Cock-a-doodle-doo.
It's morning, brothers, get up,
Cock-a-doodle-doo. Cock-a-doodle-doo'.

Tarnegol

Tarnegol, tarnegol
Kara b'kol:
Ku-ku-ri-ku ku-ku-ri-ku
Ku-ku-ri-ku ku-ku-ri-ku.
traditional Hebrew

The cock
Crows in a loud voice:
Ku-ku-ri-ku, etc.

Machli

Machli jal ki rani hai
Jeevan uska pani hai
Hath lagao dar jaigi
Bahar nikalo mar jaigi.
traditional Hindi

The fish is the queen of the water
Its whole life is water
To touch her is to scare her
Take her out and she'll surely die.

Meow meow

Billi boli meow meow
Kya mein ghar ke andar ao
Chuha bola na na na na
Mosi tum andar mat ana
traditional Hindi

The cat says miaow, miaow
Should I come inside the house?
The mouse says no no no no
Aunt, you don't come inside.

Titli

Ek phool par bathi titli
Hans ka baccho se ye boli
Pankh dekh lo, nit aungi
Tang kiya to urd jaungi.
traditional Hindi

Butterfly sitting on a flower
Smiles to the children and says,
'I'll come every day. See my wings,
If you irritate me, I'll fly away.'

Little pony

I had a little pony,
He wouldn't go anywhere,
Till he heard the Muezzin
Calling us to prayer;
Then clip-clop, clip-clop,
To the Mosque we'd go,
Summer and winter,
Sunshine or snow.

Anonymous

Pussy walks softly

Pussy walks softly on velvety paws,
You can feel them with your hand,
And touch her fur, it's soft as silk,
But her nose is rough as sand.

Barbara Ireson

A big bumblebee

A big bumblebee
Sat on a wall;
He said he could hum
And that was all.

Anonymous

A big turtle

A big turtle sat on the end of a log,
Watching a tadpole turn into a frog.

Anonymous

A white hen sitting

A white hen sitting
On white eggs three:
Nest, three speckled chickens
As plump as plump can be.

An owl, and a hawk,
And a bat come to see:
But chicks beneath their mother's wing
Squat safe as safe can be.

Christina Rossetti

Wrens and robins in the hedge

Wrens and robins in the hedge,
Wrens and robins here and there;
Building, perching, pecking, fluttering,
Everywhere!

Christina Rossetti

Ducks feeding

Ducks at the water's edge
swimming for bread
eagerly hurrying,
keen to be fed:
rare ones and common ones,
coloured and white,
with feet that are paddles
and eyes that are bright –

Smart ones and shiny ones
preening a feather,
bustling and fidgeting,
greedy together:
pretty ones, perky ones,
pushing to come,
grabbing and swallowing...

That's the last crumb!

Jean Kenward

Gulls

I went to the sea shore,
I stood upon the sand
my face to the water,
my back to the land.
I listened to the seagulls
I heard them call and cry –
they dipped to the water,
they soared to the sky.

I went to the sea shore
and nobody was there
except the tossing seagulls
that blew about the air.
I stood, and I watched them;
I heard them cry and call
with only me to answer
and no-one else at all.

Jean Kenward

Owl

Sky is dark,
No longer blue.
What's that sound?
To-whit to-whoo.

To-whit to-whoo,
Who are you?
I'm the owl,
That's who to-whoo!

Ian Larmont

Badgers

Badgers come creeping from dark under ground,
Badgers scratch hard with a bristly sound,
Badgers go nosing around.

Badgers have whiskers and black and white faces,
Badger cubs scramble and scrap and run races,
Badgers like overgrown places.

Badgers don't jump when a vixen screams,
Badgers drink quietly from moonshiny streams,
Badgers dig holes in our dreams.

Badgers are working while you and I sleep,
Pushing their tunnels down twisting and steep,
Badgers have secrets to keep.

Richard Edwards

Hunting song

The fox is in the farmyard –
Hark!
Hark!
Hark!
The foxhounds are coming –
you can hear them bark!
The people all are shouting
for to see a bit of fun –
the fox is in the farmyard!
Watch him run!

The fox is in the beech wood
Stop!
Stop!
Stop!
The hunt is up to get him
with a clip clip clop,
the hounds are out to hold him
but the fox has got away...
He's safe,
and he's secret!
HIP HOORAY!

Jean Kenward

Sea song

Splash of fish
and dart of fin,
crustacean scuttles
out and in.

Sway of frond
and flash of scale,
glimpse of silver,
flick of tail.

Shark-like shadows
gliding near:
now it's time
to disappear.

Tony Mitton

Secret

Mrs Kangaroo
Is it true,
Are you hiding
Someone new
In the pocket
Part of you?

There *must* be someone
New and growing,
His little ears
Have started showing.

Beverley McLoughland

Pupa

Brown and shiny
Like a well-polished shoe
The pupa lies.
Unearthed from its
Damp hiding place
It wriggles and squirms
In fright
Away from the light.
I wonder...
What kind of creature
Is hidden inside?

Colin Bennett

I want...

Richard owns a rabbit
Chloe's got a cat
Tricia has a terrapin
But me?
I want a *rat!*

Barry loves his budgie
Donna walks her dog
Parma rides his pony
But me?
I want a *frog!*

Harry holds his hamster
Pauline's pigeons coo
Gerry feeds his gerbil
But me?
I want a *zoo!*

Wes Magee

Lazy day

Black and white blotches by the gate,
swish a tail, stamp a hoof,
wait, wait, wait...

Sandpaper tongue, wet leather nose,
blink an eye, twitch an ear,
doze, doze, doze...

Gina Douthwaite

CLOTHES

Shoes

Red shoes, blue shoes,
Old shoes, new shoes.
Shoes that are comfy,
Shoes that are tight,
Shoes that are black,
Shoes that are white.
Shoes with buckles,
Shoes with bows,
Shoes that are narrow
And pinch your toes.
Shoes that are yellow,
Shoes that are green,
Shoes that are dirty,
Shoes that are clean.
Shoes for cold weather,
Shoes for when it's hot.
Shoes with laces
That get tangled in a knot!

John Foster

Diddle, diddle dumpling

Diddle, diddle, dumpling,
My son John
Went to bed
With his trousers on:
One shoe off,
And the other shoe on:
Diddle, diddle, dumpling,
My son John.

Anonymous

My shoes

My shoes are new and squeaky shoes,
They're very shiny, creaky shoes.
I wish I had my leaky shoes
That mother threw away.

I liked my old brown leaky shoes
Much better than these creaky shoes –
These shiny, creaky, squeaky shoes
I've got to wear today.

Anonymous

The lost shoe

Doodle doodle doo,
The princess lost her shoe;
Her highness hopped –
The fiddler stopped,
Not knowing what to do.

Anonymous

Little Betty Blue

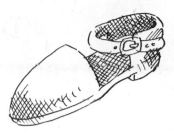

Little Betty Blue
Lost her holiday shoe;
What can little Betty do?
Give her another
To match the other,
And then she can walk out in two.

Anonymous

Mary lost her coat

Mary lost her coat,
Mary lost her hat,
Mary lost her fifty pence –
Now what do you think of that?

Mary found her coat,
Mary found her hat,
Mary found her fifty pence –
Now what do you think of that?

Anonymous

Daffy-Down-Dilly

Daffy-down-dilly is new come to town,
With a yellow petticoat, and a green gown.

Anonymous

One misty, moisty morning

One misty moisty morning,
     When cloudy was the weather,
I met a little old man
     Clothed all in leather.

He began to compliment,
     And I began to grin,
How do you do, how do you do,
     And how do you do again?

Anonymous

When I was a little girl

When I was a little girl,
     About six years old,
I hadn't got a petticoat,
     To keep me from the cold.

So I went to Darlington,
     That pretty little town,
And there I bought a petticoat,
     A cloak and a gown.

Anonymous

Which is the way?

Which is the way to London Town
To see the King in his golden crown?
One foot up and one foot down –
That's the way to London Town.

Which is the way to London Town
To see the Queen in her silken gown?
Left, right, and turn around –
Soon you'll be in London Town.

Anonymous

A little husband

I had a little husband,
No bigger than my thumb;
I put him in a pint pot
And there I bid him drum.
I bought a little horse
That galloped up and down;
I bridled him and saddled him
And sent him out of town.
I gave my husband garters
To garter up his hose,
And a little silk handkerchief,
To wipe his snotty nose.

Anonymous

Winter morning

On my cold, cold toes
are some yellow socks

on the yellow socks
are some green, green boots

on the green, green boots
is a white, white sheet

on the white, white sheet
is a warm, warm rug

and the warm, warm rug
is red, red, red!

I can hear the rain
and it's time for school...

but I'd much rather stay
in BED, BED, BED!

Judith Nicholls

Winter

When winter's wearing white,
Bright, diamond-studded dresses
She's as smiling and beguiling
As the fairest of princesses.

When winter's wearing grey,
Frayed, freezing foggy breeches
She's as vicious and capricious
As the wickedest of witches.

Cynthia Mitchell

Winter parcel

Today I'm like a parcel,
wrapped up from top to toe,
Protected from the icy winds,
the rain, the sleet and snow.

My head has got a hat on,
my neck hides in a scarf,
and on my hands some puppet gloves,
a tiger and giraffe.

My coat is thick and furry,
and does up very high.
And on my feet I've special boots,
to keep me warm and dry.

So though there's little of me
that anyone can see,
This walking, talking parcel is
most definitely ME!

Linda Hammond

Don't jump in puddles

'Don't jump
in puddles,'
said Samantha's mum;
'Remember
you're wearing
a new cardigan,
best blouse,
velvet dungarees,
pink socks,
white shoes
tied up with bows.'

But Samantha forgot,
and she ruined the lot.

Irene Rawnsley

In case you didn't know

Wellies in the summer,
Sandals in the snow,
That's the way I wear my shoes,
In case you didn't know.

Grown-ups are so funny,
Telling me I can't.
When they say, 'Go in and change!'
I just tell them, 'Shan't!'

Wellies in the summer,
Sandals in the snow,
That's the way I wear my shoes,
In case you didn't know.

Michelle Magorian

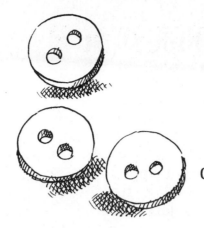

Fastening buttons

Fastening buttons,
One, two, three,
Mother's left it up to me.

Fastening buttons,
Four, five, six,
Oh those buttons do play tricks.

Fastening buttons,
Seven, eight, nine.
'Finished yet Janey?
Good, that's fine!'

Ian Larmont

Knickers

Not wearing knickers,
not navy,
no more.

Want to wear silk ones
'cause cotton's
a bore.

Want to wear pink ones
with frills. I
adore

not wearing knickers,
not navy,
no more.

Gina Douthwaite

Getting dressed

Get dressed.
Here's your vest.
A clean shirt.
I've ironed
your skirt.
Hurry up,
you'll be late!

I often wish
that I had fur,
like the cat.
Oh how I hate
getting dressed!

Ann Bonner

My old blue shirt

My old blue shirt
Is tattered and torn.
The collar is crumpled.
The elbows are worn.

The sleeve got ripped
When I climbed the tree.
There's a big dark stain
Where I spilled my tea.

But I don't care.
I like my old shirt
Though it's battered and tattered
And covered in dirt.

John Foster

New clothes

We've been to the shops.
My clothes are all new.
My shirt's really good –
it's coloured blue.

My trousers are red.
They're really great.
Can I put them on?
I just can't wait!

Charles Thomson

New clothes and old

I rather like New Clothes,
They make me feel so fine,
Yet I am not quite Me,
The clothes are not quite mine.

I really love Old Clothes,
They make me feel so free,
I know that they are mine,
For I feel just like Me.

Eleanor Farjeon

Mummy has scissors

Mummy has scissors, snip, snip, snip.
Mummy has cotton, stitch, stitch, stitch.
Mummy has buttons, one, two, three;
Mummy's making a dress
And it's just for me.

Anonymous

Safety yellow

I've a little yellow raincoat,
And a little yellow hat,
I've little yellow gumboots,
I keep them by the mat.

I wear my 'Safety Yellow'
When I'm walking in the rain,
Then everyone can see me
And I come home safe again.

Isobel Pratt

Bobble

I've got a bobble on my hat:
flip flip flop it goes.
Sometimes it topples over
and bumps into my nose!
Sometimes it bounces backwards,
sometimes it's almost still,
but it drops and plops a hundred times
when I'm running down the hill...

I've got a splendid bobble:
it's yellow, blue and red.
It's like a woollen lighthouse
shining on my head!
Sometimes, on foggy mornings,
I'm the cheeriest boy about
with a light, bright, bouncing bobble...
Bet you can't blow it out!

Jean Kenward

THROUGH THE DAY

Ten for the day

One, one,
the rising sun.

Two, two,
the sky so blue.

Three, three,
birds in the tree.

Four, four,
milk at the door.

Five, five,
the whole world alive.

Six, six,
the old clock ticks.

Seven, seven,
sun's in the heaven.

Eight, eight,
tea's on the plate.

Nine, nine,
moon starts to shine.

Ten, ten,
back to bed again.

Tony Mitton

photocopiable

Go to bed

Go to bed early – wake up with joy;
Go to bed late – cross girl or boy.
Go to bed early – ready for play;
Go to bed late – tired all day.

Go to bed early – no pains or ills;
Go to bed late – doctors and pills.
Go to bed early – grow very tall;
Go to bed late – stay very small.

Anonymous

Washing hands

Wash, hands, wash,
Johnny's gone to plough.
Splash, hands, splash,
They're all washed now.

Anonymous

I can

I can tie my shoe lace
I can comb my hair
I can wash my hands and face
And dry myself with care.

I can brush my teeth, too,
And button up my frocks;
I can say 'How do you do?'
And put on both my socks.

Anonymous

Food

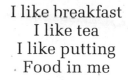
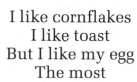

I like breakfast
I like tea
I like putting
Food in me

I like cornflakes
I like toast
But I like my egg
The most

Slice the top off
Poke about
Pull the dripping
Yolk right out

I like breakfast
I like tea
I love putting
Food in me

Tony Bradman

Letters

I like getting letters.
I like the rat tat tat.
I like the way the envelopes
tumble on the mat.

There's sure to be some excitement.
Open it quick, and see
whose is that funny writing...
Is it addressed to ME?

Jean Kenward

Nothing

Clitter clip clan
goes the Dustbin Man.
He empties the bins
as best he can.
When the lids go bowling,
hop and skip...
he runs to catch them,
clitter clan clip!

Clitter clip clan
goes the Man with a bin.
He's left us a bag
to put things in –
he's left us a bag,
but it isn't fair,
for it's full of nothing –
there's NOTHING in there!

Jean Kenward

Down by the river

Down by the river
Where the green grass grows,
There sits Mary washing her clothes.
She sings, she sings, she sings so sweet
And calls to her playmates up and down
the street.

Patrick, Patrick,
Won't you come to tea?
Come next Sunday at half past three.
Tea cakes, pancakes
and everything you see –
Oh we'll have a jolly time
At half past three.

Anonymous

Mr Nobody

I know a funny little man,
As quiet as a mouse,
Who does the mischief that is done
In everybody's house.
There's no-one ever sees his face,
And yet we all agree
That every plate we break was cracked
By Mr Nobody.

The finger marks upon the door,
By none of us are made;
We never leave the curtains closed,
Or leave the bed unmade;
The ink we never spill; the boots
That lying round you see
Are not our boots; they all belong
To Mr Nobody.

Anonymous

Sick

Hot, cross, aching head,
Prickly, tickly, itchy head.
Piles of books and toys and puzzles
Heavy on my feet,
Pillows thrown all anyhow,
Wrinkles in the sheet.
Sick of medicine, lemonade,
Soup spooned from a cup.
When will I be *better?*
When can I *get up?*

Shirley Hughes

Sympathy

I've got a cut
just here on my knee.
It's ever so small
so it's hard to see.
But I hope you'll be nice and kind to me
'cos I've got a cut, just here – see?

I've got a graze
just here on my toe
and how I got it
I just don't know.
But it's hurting a bit, and bleeding, so
I hope you'll be kind to me.

I've got a tummy-ache in my head.
My mummy has sent me back to bed.
Well, lucky for me, I'm not quite dead,
but I hope she'll be kind to me.

I've got this and I've got that
and I only want a hug and a chat
and all I'm really hoping is that
they'll all be nice to me.

Tony Mitton

Yellow

Yellow for melons.
Yellow for sun.
Yellow for buttercups,
Picked one by one.

The yolk of an egg
Is yellow, too.
And sometimes clouds
Have a daffodil hue.

Bananas are yellow
And candleshine.
What's your favourite colour?
Yellow is mine.

Olive Dove

The paint box

Peacock, peony,
violet, jade –
these are the colours
I like made;

Sunflower yellow,
deep sea blue,
green, like a wheatfield
pushing through,

Orange, crimson,
amber, jet,
and the four
I won't forget –

Peacock, peony,
violet, jade...
Nobody knows
how magic's made.

Jean Kenward

Packed lunch

Lunchbox, lunchbox,
What's in my lunchbox?
What's for lunch today?

Brown rolls, chewy,
Cream cheese, gooey,
Cucumber crunchy,
Carrot sticks munchy,

And a big rosy apple –

Hurray!

Jill Bennett

Tea time

First, the tea bag in the pot,
Fill with water, boiling hot.
Leave five minutes, maybe four,
Then it's time for him to pour.

Milk and sugar in the cup.
Lift the pot and fill it up.
Then I've got a cup of tea.
Made by Daddy, made for me.

Ian Larmont

Tea trouble

My baby brother wouldn't eat
anything for tea,
so Mummy told him to pretend
he was a monster from the sea.
Then he ate a banana boat
with a bread and butter sail,
but I was in trouble when I drank
my milk like a killer whale!

Robin Mellor

Jam

Oh, what a disgrace,
there's jam on my face,
there's jam on my nose and my knee.
There's jam on the floor,
there's jam on the door,
and it's all 'cos we've got jam for tea.

There's jam on the mat,
there's jam on the cat,
there's jam over you and on me.
There's jam on the pram,
there's jam on me mam,
it must be a jam jamboree.

There's jam on my hair,
there's jam everywhere,
but the thing that upsets me the most,
is there's jam to be found,
and it's spread all around,
but I can't get the jam on my toast.

Tony Mitton

The soap fish

Soap is just soap
when it sits on the dish,
but when in the bath
it becomes like a fish.

And when the soap
with your fingers you feel,
it scuds like a squid
and it slips like an eel.

Then off through the water
it flicks like a fin.
It teases your toes
and it tickles your skin.

Tony Mitton

Hairwashing

Long or short,
dark or fair,
everyone has to
wash their hair.

Run the water,
fetch shampoo,
make a lather,
oh, boo hoo!

Please don't shriek,
please don't howl,
shut your eyes,
here's the towel.

Brushing's over,
switch off drier:
milk and biscuits
by the fire.

Tony Mitton

There's a spider in my bath!

I can't see his web,
I can't see any flies.
I wonder what he eats all day
to make him such a size?

I can't see his mouth,
I can't see his eyes.
I wonder *how* he eats each day
to make him such a size?

Judith Nicholls

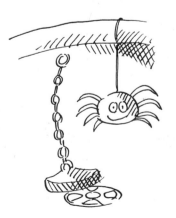

Fire

Fire is a dragon
(Better beware),
Dangerous and beautiful
(Better take care).
Puffing out smoke
As soon as it's lit,
Licking up leaves,
Crackle and spit!
Sending up sparks
Into the sky
That hover a moment
And suddenly die.
Fire is a dragon,
Alive in the night;
Fiery dragon,
Glittering bright.

Shirley Hughes

Where?

Where do I feel free? Up high
in the apple tree with its creak and sigh.

Where do I feel scared? Down deep
in burrows and tunnels where blind things creep.

Where do I feel safe? In bed
when my teddy's there and my prayers are said.

Sue Cowling

How?

How did the sun get up in the sky?
– A billy goat tossed it up too high,
Said my Uncle.

How did the stars get up there too?
– They're sparks from the thunder-horse's shoe,
Said my Uncle.

And tell me about the moon as well.
– The moon jumped out of an oyster shell,
Said my Uncle.

And how did the oceans get so deep?
– I'll tell you tomorrow. Now go to sleep,
Said my Uncle.

Richard Edwards

Peace

When I close my eyes,
Peace comes alive,
And takes me as a shadow.
We travel above,
On a cloud sprinkling love,
That washes away all sorrow.

Vyanne Samuels

Sunshine at bedtime

Streets full of blossom,
Like pink and white snow,
Beds full of tulips,
Tucked in a row.

Trees full of 'candles'
Alight in the park,
Sunshine at bedtime,
Why isn't it dark?

Yet high in the sky
I saw the moon,
Pale as a ghost
In the afternoon.

Shirley Hughes

Sandmen, sandmen

Sandmen, sandmen,
Wise and creepy,
Croon dream-songs
To make us sleepy.
A lovely maid with deep dark eyes
Is queen of all their lullabies.
On her ancient moon-guitar
She strums a sleep-song to a star;
And when the deep dark shadows fall
Snow-white lilies hear her call.
Sandmen, sandmen,
Wise and creepy,
Croon dream-songs
To make us sleepy.

Anonymous

Night lights

There is no need to light a night-light
On a light night like tonight;
For a night-light's light's a slight light
When the moon's white and bright.

Anonymous

Twinkle, twinkle

Twinkle, twinkle, little star,
How I wonder what you are.
Up above the world so high,
Like a diamond in the sky.

When the blazing sun has gone,
When it nothing shines upon,
Then you show your little light,
Twinkle, twinkle all the night.

Anonymous

The moon shines bright

The moon shines bright,
The stars give light,
And little Nanny Button-Cap
Will come tomorrow night.

Anonymous

Star light

Star light, star bright,
First star I see tonight,
I wish I may, I wish I might,
Have the wish I wish tonight.

Anonymous

A piece of sun

I'll take a piece of sun
and I'll take a piece of moon,
a droplet from the ocean deep
for I'll be going soon.
And then into my rucksack
I'll put a grain of sand –
And these will be my magic charms
till I reach that far off land.

Philip de Vos

Star song

I saw a star
in the midnight sky...
Far, (how far!)
it journeyed by,
more than a million
miles away
bright with the glint
of yesterday.

I saw the moon
beside it keep
an open eye
that could not sleep –
could not close,
nor wink a bit
till came a cloud
and covered it.

I saw the moon,
I saw the star
sail together
far, (how far!)
On and on
and further yet...

Did I sleep, then?
I forget.

Jean Kenward

FAMILY AND FRIENDS

What are friends like?

Friends are kind,
Friends are fun,
Friends can talk and listen too,
Friends can help,
Friends can hug,
You like them and they like you.

Friends can share,
Friends can care,
Friends can play with you all day,
Friends say sorry,
Friends forgive,
Friends don't sulk or run away.

Friends are good,
Friends are great,
Friends can laugh and joke with you,
Friends are true,
Friends are fond,
Friends enjoy the things you do.

I like friends, don't you?

Ruth Kirtley

Someone

Someone
to talk with,
to dance with,
to sing with,
to eat with,
to laugh with,
to cry with,
to think with,
to understand –
someone...
to be my friend.

Susan Schutz

Sally

Sally didn't
come to school
today.
Sally had
an accident,
I heard
my teacher say.

It might be
several weeks
till she is better.
We all
made cards
and teacher
wrote a letter.

I felt quite
sad and quiet
all afternoon.
I said
a prayer
that she'll
get better soon.

Charles Thomson

Together, whatever the weather

Together we
splash in the rain,
crunch in the snow,
spin in the wind,
stumble in the dark,
and laugh in the sun.
Together,
together,
together.
Whatever,
whatever,
the weather!

Ian Souter

Who?

Who
will
never leave
always play
never hide
always stay
at my side
every day
...?
My
pretend
friend!

Judith Nicholls

Let's talk

Lips are for speaking
And smiling too,
Tongues are for saying
How do you do?

Hands are for waving
To people on the street
And hearts are for loving
Everyone we meet.

Ask the person on your left
If he would be your friend
Then turn to your right
And do the same again.

Telcine Turner

Comforting thought

The silence of rabbit
The snuggle of cat
The warmth of a cushion
Where somebody's sat.

Hiawyn Oram

Friend

My friend broke the window.
My friend lost the ball.
My friend took the crayons
And scribbled on the wall.

My friend is so naughty.
My friend's not like me.
That friend is my best friend
the one I can't see.

Ann Bonner

Kandy Blue and Balaballoo

Kandy Blue and Balaballoo,
have lots of friends just like you.
Ali the elephant big, and rare
and cuddly Dudley
who must be a bear.
Koki the tiger
and right beside her
Rilli the monkey,
ever so hungry,
and Mongo the mongoose
who loves mango juice,
and parrots and carrots
and bright red shoes.

Kandy Blue,
and Balaballoo,
have all these friends
and many more too.

Romesh Gunesekera

Goodnight

When I climb into bed and snuggle up tight,
I know that I'll want to say goodnight
to hippo, to seal and to polar bear,
to the fluffy dog that I won at the fair,
to the photo of dad in the frame by my bed,
to my monkey, my mouse and my one-eyed ted,
to my old elephant with a tear in its tum,
and an extra special goodnight to my Mum!

Brian Moses

My teddy bear

My old bear can keep secrets,
he's a best friend to me,
we sleep together in the same bed
and share our cups of tea.

His fur is worn and rough now
and his eyes have lost their gleam,
but he holds me close and comforts me
when I wake from a frightening dream.

If ever he were to be bearnapped
I'd give everything I own,
all my toys and money – anything,
to get my bear back home.

No, I won't put him in the cupboard
and I don't want a new teddy bear;
he may be old, torn and tattered
but I love him, so I don't care.

Robin Mellor

Ted

I'm old and I've only one glass eye.
My ears are floppy and torn.
The stuffing has crumbled in my legs
And my fur is bare and worn.

But I'll always go wherever you go.
I'll snuggle up close in bed.
You can count on me to look after you.
I'm your very own special Ted.

John Foster

Water everywhere

There's water on the ceiling,
And water on the wall,
There's water in the bedroom,
And water in the hall,
There's water on the landing,
And water on the stair,
Whenever Daddy takes a bath
There's water everywhere.

Valerie Bloom

This morning my dad shouted

This morning my dad shouted.
This morning my dad swore.
There was water through the ceiling.
There was water on the floor.
There was water on the carpets.
There was water down the stairs.
The kitchen stools were floating
So were the dining chairs.

This morning I've been crying.
Dad made me so upset.
He shouted and he swore at me
Just 'cause things got so wet.
I only turned the tap on
To get myself a drink.
The trouble is I didn't see
The plug was in the sink.

John Foster

Who did it?

Who put pudding
in dad's best black shoes?

Me.

Who put jelly
in his umbrella?

Me.

Who put a spider
in his bowler hat
and stuffed his briefcase
full of old comics?

Me.

then go to bed
without any tea.

Irene Rawnsley

Kiss me quick

Kiss me quick, mum,
I can't wait,
My friend is standing
At the gate.

Kiss me quick, mum,
I must fly,
All my friends
Are going by.

Kiss me quick, mum,
Don't be slow...
I must be off now –
Cheerio!

Tony Bradman

What is under?

What is under the grass, Mummy,
what is under the grass?
Roots and stones and rich soil
where the loamy worms pass.

What is over the sky, Mummy,
what is over the sky?
Stars and planets and boundless space,
but never a reason why.

What is under the sea, Mummy,
what is under the sea?
Weird and wet and wondrous things,
too deep for you and me.

What is under my skin, Mummy,
what is under my skin?
Flesh and blood and a frame of bones
and your
own dear self within.

Tony Mitton

Vanessa or the lucky egg

My mum told me that right inside
Her tummy there have been
A million, billion tiny eggs,
So small they can't be seen.

And every month they come and go,
But just occasionally
One grows into a baby,
And is born like you and me.

You cannot tell which one will grow,
Or what sort it will be,
There might be more than one, like twins,
or triplets if there's three.

Mum could have had a baby Tom,
A baby Ann or Fred,
But she had me, Vanessa
Wasn't I a lucky egg!

Theresa Heine

Me!

Mum says,
I mustn't charge down the stairs any more,
I mustn't slide across the slippery, kitchen floor,
I mustn't be cheeky or ever rude
or just eat sweets for all my food
because I belong to her.

Dad says,
I mustn't cross busy roads all on my own,
I mustn't hang around on my way home.
I mustn't get wet and catch a cold
in fact I must do everything I am told
because I belong to him.

But I say,
I want to do what I want to do
SOMETIMES!
because I belong to ME!

Ian Souter

I had a little brother

I had a little brother
No bigger than my thumb.

I put him in the coffee-pot.
He rattled like a drum.

I had a little sister
No bigger than a flea.

I put her in the milk-jug
Then poured her in my tea.

Anonymous

When Susie eats custard

When Susie eats custard,
It splashes everywhere –
Down her bib, up her nose,
All over her high chair.

She pokes it with her fingers.
She spreads it on her hair.
When Susie's eating custard,
She gets it everywhere.

John Foster

Potty, but true

My little baby sister
Spends hours on the pot,
Smiling on her plastic throne –
But she doesn't do a lot.

Mum and Dad sit waiting,
While baby sister wriggles;
But she produces nothing,
Except some burps and giggles.

Mum and Dad look worried,
It shows up all their wrinkles;
But still my little sister
Just won't provide those tinkles.

Mum and Dad try very hard,
They always promise treats;
If she would only fill the pot
They'd buy her toys and sweets.

But I could tell them something
They really ought to know;
The second that she's off the pot,
That's when she's *bound* to go!

Tony Bradman

Foot marching

Sometimes I stand on Grandad's feet
And he walks round the floor,
And he sings me ancient army songs
He picked up in the war.
Sometimes we go backwards,
And sometimes round-about,
I never, ever let him stop
Until he's worn me out.

Jean Willis

Polishing Grandad

Grandad's got no hair.
He's got a shiny head.
Because there's nothing
There to brush,
I polish him instead.

Jean Willis

Uncle Paul

My Uncle Paul makes lots and lots
Of extra-ordinary pots.
I only wish one day he'd choose
To make a pot that we could *use*.

Colin West

Granny Brigg's baking day

When Granny Briggs has a baking day,
Into the oven goes tray after tray
Of scones and buns, jam tarts and cakes –
All the delicious things she bakes.

She puts some dough in a bowl by the fire
And I can watch it rise higher and higher,
Then she makes lovely crusty bread,
'Home-made's best,' so Granny Briggs said.

Daphne Lister

Granny's alarm

When Granny fell
And broke her arm,
She pressed the knob
On her alarm.

It's nice to know,
That when she's ill,
If we can't help
Then someone will.

Janis Priestley

Reflections

I look in the mirror
And what do I see?
I see my twin sister.
She's looking at me.

We both look the same
In the clothes that we wear.
The same colour eyes
And the same colour hair.

I look in the mirror
And what do I see?
It's not my twin sister.
I'm looking at me.

Wendy Larmont

My Aunty Maisie!

When my Aunty Maisie,
has been a little forgetful,
a little hazy,

A little mixed-up,
a little mazy,

A little slow,
even a little lazy,

She always says,
'Whoops a daisy!'

That's my hazy, mazy, sometimes lazy
Aunty Maisie.
She drives me CRAZY!

Ian Souter

FOOD

The apple tree

As I went up the apple tree
All the apples fell on me;
Bake a pudding, bake a pie,
Send it up to John Mackay;
John Mackay is not in,
Send it to the man in the moon.

Anonymous

As I went up the apple tree

As I went up the apple tree,
All the apples fell on me;
Bake a pudding, bake a pie,
Did you ever tell a lie?
Yes you did, you know you did,
You broke your grandma's teapot lid.

Anonymous

photocopiable

Apple crumble

I like apple crumble –
it sticks onto the spoon.
I'd eat it every morning
and every afternoon,
I'd eat it for my breakfast,
for supper, lunch or tea...
yes, I like apple crumble:
Just pass me some, and see!

Apple crumble's
Fine and tasty.
Apple crumble's
nice.
You can serve it
hot and steamy
or as cold
as ice.
You can swallow it
in pieces
and in dollops
too;
you can gulp it,
chew it, bite it
like the tigers
do.
You can have it
smooth and creamy,
crisp and brown
on top –
GO on making
apple crumble!
Never, never
stop,
for I couldn't
and I wouldn't
say 'No thank you'...
WHAT?
You're not baking
ANY pudding?
Did you say
you're NOT?

Jean Kenward

Humpty Dumpty's fruit pie

Apple, orange, strawberry, pear,
grapefruit, kiwi, lemon and plum;
bilberry, blackberry, pineapple, fig,
eat them all up if you want to grow BIG!

Judith Nicholls

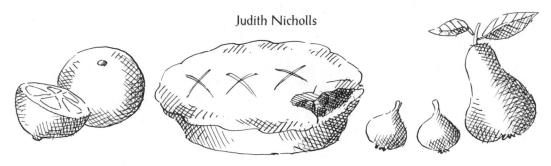

A lucky bag dip

Barley sugar,
Chocolate drops,
Peppermint creams
And lollipops,
Treacle toffee,
Candyfloss,
Liquorice allsorts,
Bonbon BOSS.

Cynthia Mitchell

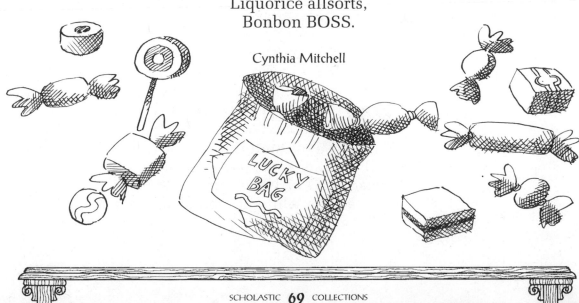

Polly

Polly put the kettle on,
Sally blow the bellows strong,
Molly call the muffin man,
We'll all have tea.

Anonymous

Charlie Wag

Charlie Wag,
Charlie Wag,
Ate the pudding
And left the bag.

Anonymous

Hannah Bantry

Hannah Bantry,
In the pantry,
Gnawing at a mutton bone;
How she gnawed it,
How she clawed it,
When she found herself alone.

Anonymous

Davy Dumpling

Davy Davy Dumpling,
Boil him in the pot;
Sugar him and butter him,
And eat him while he's hot.

Anonymous

The pasty

Deedle deedle dumpling, my son John,
Ate a pasty five feet long;
He bit it once, he bit it twice,
Oh, my goodness, it was full of mice!

Anonymous

Betty Botter's butter

Betty Botter bought some butter,
But, she said, the butter's bitter;
If I put it in my batter
It will make my batter bitter,
But a bit of better butter,
That would make my batter better.
So she bought a bit of butter
Better than her bitter butter,
And she put it in her batter
And the batter was not bitter.
So t'was better Betty Botter
Bought a bit of better butter.

Anonymous

Baby and I

Baby and I
Were baked in a pie,
The gravy was wonderful hot.
We had nothing to pay
To the baker that day
And so we crept out of the pot.

Anonymous

Clap hand for mammy

Clap hand for mammy
Till daddy come,
Daddy bring cake and sugarplum
Give baby some.

Baby eat all
Ain't give mammy none,
Mammy get vex
Throw baby down.

traditional Caribbean

Ten biscuits

Ten biscuits
In a pack
Who don't want dem
Turn their back.

Back-to-back
Sago-pap
Ten biscuits
In a pack.

traditional Caribbean

Jolly red nose

Nose, nose,
Jolly red nose,
And what gave thee
That jolly red nose?
Nutmeg and ginger,
Cinnamon and cloves,
That's what gave me
This jolly red nose.

Anonymous

Mangoes

Mangoes ripe an' juicy,
Hangin' from de tree,
Mangoes ripe an' ready,
Go pick one for me.

Pawpaws ripe an' juicy,
Hangin' from de tree,
Pawpaws ripe an' ready,
Go pick one for me.

traditional Caribbean

My mammy's maid

Dingty diddlety,
My mammy's maid,
She stole oranges,
I am afraid;
Some in her pocket,
Some in her sleeve,
She stole oranges,
I do believe

Anonymous

Poll Parrot

Little Poll Parrot
Sat in his garret
Eating toast and tea;
A little brown mouse
Jumped into the house
And stole it all away.

Anonymous

A peanut

A peanut sat on the railroad track
His heart was all a-flutter.
Along came a train – the 5:15 –
Toot, toot, peanut butter.

Anonymous

To the bat

Bat, bat, come under my hat,
And I'll give you a slice of bacon;
And when I bake, I'll give you a cake,
If I am not mistaken.

Anonymous

Three little ghostesses

Three little ghostesses
Sitting on postesses
Eating buttered toastesses
Creasing their wristesses
Up to their fistesses
Oh what beastesses
To make such feastesses.

Anonymous

Pease pudding

Pease pudding hot,
Pease pudding cold,
Pease pudding in the pot
Nine days old.
Some like it hot,
Some like it cold,
Some like it in the pot
Nine days old.

Anonymous

Peas

I eat my peas with honey,
I've done it all my life.
It makes the peas taste funny,
But it keeps them on the knife.

Anonymous

Jelly wobbles

When jelly doubles
Everyone bubbles.
When jelly quivers
Everyone shivers.
When jelly wiggles
Everyone giggles.
When jelly shakes
Everyone quakes.
But WHEN JELLY WOBBLES
EVERYONE GOBBLES!

Ian Souter

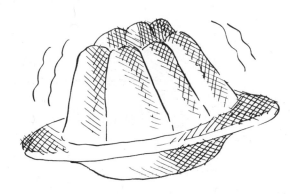

Today for lunch!

Today for lunch I had –
10 sizzling spoonfuls of specially spiced soup,
9 beautiful bites of brown baked bread,
8 chewy chunks of crispy, crinkly chips,
7 black bits of burnt baked beans,
6 terrific titbits of tasty tender tomatoes,
5 fat fingers of freshly fried fish,
4 pleasing pieces of perfect pecan pie,
3 creamy cups of cool clotted cream,
2 jumbo jars of juicy jolly jelly
which left me with
1 big bulge of bursting burping belly!

Ian Souter

Jenny

Hie to the market, Jenny come trot,
Spilt all her buttermilk, every drop,
Every drop and every dram,
Jenny came home with an empty can.

Anonymous

To market

To market, to market,
To buy a plum bun;
Home again, home again,
Market is done.

Anonymous

Little girl

Little girl, little girl,
Where have you have been?
I've been to see grandmother
Over the green.
What did she give you?
Milk in a can.
What did you say for it?
Thank you, Grandam.

Anonymous

Jack-a-Dandy

Nauty Pauty Jack-a-Dandy
Stole a piece of sugar candy
From the grocer's shoppy-shop,
And away did hoppy-hop.

Anonymous

Cakes and custard

When Jacky's a good boy,
He shall have cakes and custard;
But when he does nothing but cry,
He shall have nothing but mustard.

Anonymous

Bread Man! Bread Man!

Bread Man! Bread Man!
Have you any bread?
Yes son! Yes son!
Three rolls of bread;
One for your family,
One for the school and
One for that poor old man
Who lives with his mule.

Anonymous

The turnip

Mr Finney had a turnip,
And it grew, and it grew,
And it grew behind the barn,
And the turnip did no harm.

And it grew, and it grew
Till it could grow no taller,
And Mr Finney took it
And he put it in the cellar.

There it lay, there it lay
Till it began to rot,
And his daughter Lizzie took it
And she put it in the pot.

And she boiled it, and she boiled it
As long as she was able,
And his daughter Susie took it
And she put it on the table.

Mr Finney and his wife
Both sat down to sup,
And they ate, and they ate,
And they ate the turnip up!

Anonymous

I don't like custard

I don't like custard
I don't like custard

Sometimes it's lumpy
sometimes it's thick
I don't care what it's like
It always makes me sick

I don't like custard
I don't like custard

Don't want it on my pie
don't want it on my cake
don't want it on my pudding
don't want it on my plate

I don't like custard
I don't like custard

It dribbles on the table
It dribbles on the floor
It sticks on your fingers
Then it sticks to the door

I don't like custard
I don't like custard

I can't eat it slowly
I can't eat it quick
Any way I eat it
It always makes me sick

I don't like custard
I don't like custard

Michael Rosen

Ogre

I like cabbage
I like plums
I like everything
that comes.

I like minnows
I like whales,
I like a tool bag
full of nails,

I like snow
and I like ice –
I could eat
a mountain, twice.

I like rubbish,
boxes, bins,
empty bottles,
knitting pins.

I like gravel,
I like stones,
I like a heap of
elephants' bones.

I can eat
as much as ten –
half the world,
and half again:

If all the seas
were in one cup,
I could swallow –
and drink them up!

Jean Kenward

Chanda mama (Uncle Moon)

Chanda mama door day
Purrai pakae boor day
Aap khaway thali which
Monai na day piali which
Piali gai toot, nona gia roos.
Nawi piali liawan gay,
Monai na manawan gay.
Aassi doodh malai khaawan gay
Chanda mama door day.
traditional Punjabi

Chanda mama door ke
Khoe pakaye boor ke
Aap khaaye thali mein
Munne ko de pyali mein
Pyali gaye toot, munna gaya rooth
Nai piali lian ghay
Munne ko manaayenge
Doodh malai khayenge
Chanda mama door ke.
traditional Hindi

Uncle Moon is far away
As we eat pancake
From a tray
The little boy is eating
From a china bowl
the bowl breaks
the boy sulks
We will buy a new one
To comfort him
And he will eat his milk and cream.

Ninny babba ninny

Ninny babba ninny,
Rhothi mucken chinny,
Roti mucken hogiah,
Meyra babba sogiah.
traditional Punjabi

Sleep baby sleep,
Bread butter sugar,
Bread butter eaten up,
My baby's gone to sleep.

Rayri wallah geet

Gurum unday gurum unday,
gurum unday gurum unday.
Ke-le Ke-le Ke-le Ke-le.
Cholay masahlay, cholay masahlay,
Cholay masahlay, cholay masahlay
Cha cha cha cha cha,
Cha cha cha cha cha.
traditional Punjabi (street cry)

gurum unday – hot eggs
ke-le – bananas
chollay masahlay – chick peas and herbs
cha – tea

Avatiach

Avatiach agol agol,
Avatiach gadol gadol,
Gadol, gadol, gadol,
Agol, agol, agol.
traditional Hebrew

A watermelon, round, round,
A watermelon, large, large,
Large, large, large,
Round, round, round.

The Mouse, the Frog, and the Little Red Hen

Once a Mouse, a Frog, and a Little Red Hen
Together kept a house;
The Frog was the laziest of frogs,
And lazier still was the Mouse.

The work all fell on the Little Red Hen,
Who had to get the wood,
And build the fires, and scrub, and cook,
And sometimes hunt for food.

One day, as she went scratching round,
She found a bag of rye;
Said she, 'Now who will make some bread?'
Said the lazy Mouse, 'Not I.'

'Nor I,' croaked the Frog as he drowsed in the shade,
Red Hen made no reply,
But flew around with bowl and spoon,
And mixed and stirred the rye.

'Who'll make the fire to bake the bread?'
Said the Mouse again, 'Not I,'
And scarcely op'ning his sleepy eyes,
Frog made the same reply.

The Little Red Hen said never a word,
But a roaring fire she made;
And while the bread was baking brown,
'Who'll set the table?' she said.

'Not I,' said the sleepy Frog with a yawn;
'Nor I,' said the Mouse again.
So the table she set, and the bread put on,
'Who'll eat this bread?' said the Hen.

'I will!' cried the Frog. 'And I!' squeaked the Mouse
As they near the table drew:
'Oh, no, you won't!' said the Little Red Hen,
And away with the loaf she flew.

Anonymous

HOMES

I know a little house

I know a little house,
With walls, one, two, three, four;
With ivy climbing up them,
And roses round the door.
It's got four little windows
With shutters open wide
And a lovely windy staircase,
That goes up and up inside.
There's a roof with a crooked chimney,
And in the garden a tree so tall,
That if you were to climb it,
You'd see over the garden wall.

Valerie McCarthy

Mother Goose's house

Mother Goose had a house,
'Twas built in a wood,
Where an owl at the door
For sentinel stood.

Anonymous

Nothing-at-all

There was an old woman called
Nothing-at-all,
Who lived in a dwelling exceedingly
small;
A man stretched his mouth to its
utmost extent,
And down in one gulp house and old
woman went.

Anonymous

There was an old woman lived under a hill

There was an old woman lived under a hill
And if she's not gone, she lives there still,
Baked apples she sold, and cranberry pies,
And she's the old woman who never told lies.

Anonymous

The crooked man

There was a crooked man,
and he walked a crooked mile,
He found a crooked sixpence
against a crooked stile;
He bought a crooked cat,
which caught a crooked mouse.
And they all lived together
in a little crooked house.

Anonymous

The old woman and her shoe

There was an old woman who lived in a shoe,
She had so many children
she didn't know what to do;
She gave them some broth without any bread;
Put their feet in hot water and sent them to bed.

Anonymous

The hat of the house

Houses have roofs like hats
To keep out rain and snow
And cover their heads
When strong winds blow.

From under the hat of the house
Windows stare like eyes
At the passing clouds
And wink at the sun in the sky.

Through the hat of the house
The chimneys stick
Like long red ears
Made out of brick.

On the hat of the house
Tired birds take a rest
Or under its edges
Build their nests.

Holes for ears
And birds' nests in a hat –
Not many people
Have hats like that!

Stanley Cook

Living-places

Where do you live?

The whole world over
People live in different places –
Up on a mountain, down by a river,
In crowded cities, or open spaces,
In houses, in flats, in tents, or trailers,
Underground, on the ground, high in the air,
Where it's hot, where it's cold, where it's dry or raining.

Millions of people live everywhere.

Julie Norman

Homes

What sort of home
have YOU got?
A tent?
A flat?
A house?
Did you build the walls
with bits of straw
and paper, like
a mouse?

What sort of roof
have YOU got?
Canvas?
Tile?
Or thatch?
And what will you do
if a wolf or two
comes sniffing
by the latch?

Jean Kenward

Inside my own house

Inside my own house.
Inside my own bedroom.
Inside my own wardrobe.
Inside my own darkness
hides:–

a long, woolly scarf,
a thick, duffle-coat,
a single, odd shoe,
a green, waterproof jacket,
a red, muddy wellington,
an odd, stripy sock,
a forgotten, broken toy,
a flat, punctured ball,
a red pair of shorts
(and when I've been told off
then sent to my room),
a sulky, bad tempered ME!

Ian Souter

I live in a hut

I live in a hut
on the top of a hill
and no one can see me
or hear me until
I open the door
and put on the light
in my hut on the top of the hill.

I live in a hut
with my dog and no friend.
I take care of myself
and no one can send
me to school or to work –
I just stay out of sight
in my hut with a dog and no friend.

Nancy Chambers

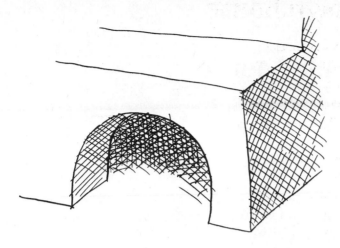

Mouse

Mouse! Mouse!
There's a mouse in my house –
squeak
      squeak
            squeak!
Little and spare
I've heard him there
now every night
for a week!

It's scuttle and fidget
and nibble, and then
a sort of rustling
            sound
as if he were scrabbling
round about –
and what can it be
      he's found?

Mouse! Mouse!
there's a mouse in my house...
He's somewhere
      I suppose,
with a tail as thin
as a length of string...
but where do you guess
                  he goes?

Jean Kenward

All alone

I'm all alone in the house
Except for the mouse
Whose hole is under the stair,
And the sounds that I hear
All fill me with fear
As I sit here in my chair.

There's no one there
But I hear the squeaking of a
door.
There's no one there
But I hear a board creak in the
floor.
There's no one there
But I hear someone calling me...

I'm alone in the house
Except for the mouse
Whose hole is under the stair,
And the sounds that I hear
All fill me with fear
As I sit here in my chair.

Barbara Ireson & Chris Rowe

Bobby Bottle Mouse

Brown Bobby Bottle Mouse
lived in a bottle house;
along came the sunshine
to warm his little day.

Along came the raindrops
to wash his little windows,
along came the wind
and blew his house away.

Brown Bobby Bottle Mouse
rolled in his bottle house
down to the river
where the fishes swim;

down to the harbour,
saw the boats a-bobbing;
down to the sea
where a shark saw him.

Brave Bobby Bottle Mouse
safe inside his bottle house
sailed with the seabird,
lucky as could be.

Sailed away to France
in his own little bottle boat;
said to the shark,
'You can't catch me!'

Brown Bobby Bottle Mouse
landed in his bottle house
high on the shore
when the moon shone bright.

A mouse with an accordian
crept in beside him;
they still live together
singing songs every night.

Irene Rawnsley

Little King Boggen

Little King Boggen,
He built a fine hall.
Pie-crust and pastry-crust,
That was the wall;
The windows were made of
Black puddings and white;
The roof was of pancakes –
You n'er saw the like.

Anonymous

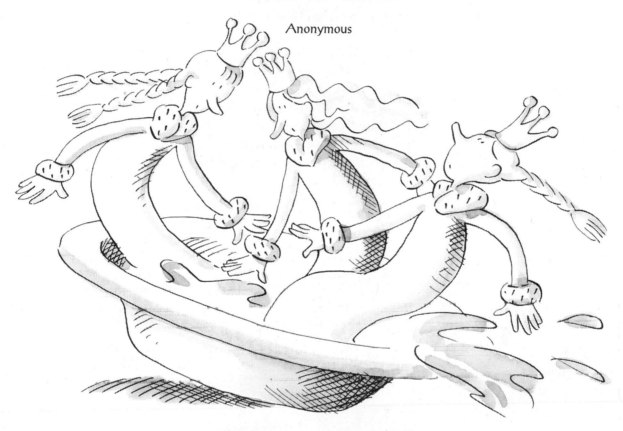

There was a king

There was a king, and he had three daughters,
And they all lived in a basin of water;
The basin bended,
My story's ended.
If the basin had been stronger,
My story would have been longer.

Anonymous

'The Seashell'

I know an old lady,
(But not very well),
And she lives in a house
That's called 'The Seashell'.
Inside there are stairs
Curling round, up so high,
You think you are on
Your way to the sky!
The house gets smaller
Nearer the top
And up in the attic
The curly stairs stop.
So it *is* like a shell
In a kind of a way,
But you can't see the sea
Though the old lady says
When you're curled up in bed –
If you don't snore –
You can hear the sea whispering
Down on the shore.

Daphne Lister

Take two cushions

Take two cushions,
And a chair,
Put them together,
Anywhere.

Add a blanket,
And a rug,
This is my house,
Nice and snug.

Find my tea-set,
Fetch it all,
Then I'll ask my friends
to call.

Tony Bradman

This is my little house

This is my little house,
(Indicate a roof by putting fingers together.)
This is the door.
(Hold tips of index fingers together.)
The windows are shining
(Pretend to polish the windows.)
And so is the floor.
(Pretend to polish the floor.)
Outside there is a chimney
(Hold hands up high for the chimney.)
As tall as can be,
With smoke that goes curling up.
(Wave one hand slowly above head.)
Come and see.

Anonymous

Jolly Roger lived up a tree

Jolly Roger lived up a tree,
You climbed there by a rope.
I'd often go for a cup of tea,
Which he brewed up with some soap.

One day I found a sock in mine,
It made me choke a bit.
But Roger said, 'Well, never mind.
It's old and doesn't fit.'

Anonymous

Tree

bird home
leaf home
ant home
lizard home
twig
branch
caterpillar
home

seed shade
sheep shade
cow shade
horse shade
wallaby shade
people shade
ground shade
sun shade

a tree is a green umbrella
with brown bits

Jenny Boult

Night lights

My bedroom's at the very top
And when I am in bed
The buses from the street outside
Throw lights above my head.

They glide along my ceiling,
Sometimes fast and sometimes slow,
And I think of all the people
In the bus that's passed below.

And when it's dark and I can't sleep
I lie back and pretend
That every light crossing my room
Is a secret night-time friend.

Michelle Magorian

Stamp stamp stamp

You can hide in our house
you can make a camp
you can march all around our house
stamp stamp stamp

Michael Rosen

Three taps

A silver tap
fills the red bowl
in the kitchen sink.

A golden tap
drips in our bathroom.
Plink.
Plonk.
Plink.

A rusty tap
dribbles by the garden wall
and gives the birds a drink.

Wes Magee

Help, it's raining!

The great grey slug
hides under a stone;
I think *I'd* rather be a snail
and hide in my own home!

Judith Nicholls

The old house

They're pulling down
the old house today:
they're making a road
and it stands in the way.

Mummy says it's a crime
that she can't forgive.
I cried – it was where
we used to live.

Charles Thomson

NONSENSE

Inside your house

Inside your house
you will find
a blue beetle boxing,
a crimson centipede cuddling,
an emerald earwig eating,
a golden grasshopper gulping,
a scarlet spider snoring,
inside your house,
inside your house.

Inside your house
you will find
an amber ant acting,
a damson dragonfly dancing,
a fawn fly fighting,
a maroon millipede mumbling,
a white worm wriggling,
inside your house,
inside your house.

Wes Magee

photocopiable

Susie Susie

Susie, Susie suck your toe
All the way to Mexico
When you get there, cut your hair,
And don't forget your underwear.

traditional USA

As I was going

As I was going up the stair
I met a man who wasn't there.
He wasn't there again today,
I wish that man would go away!

Anonymous

Froggles

Froggles live in boggles
and Toadles live in hoadles,
they swimble in the pondle
and happle they all be.

Robin Mellor

Ooey Gooey

Ooey Gooey was a worm,
Ooey Gooey loved to squirm.
Squirmed up on the railway track,
Squirmed around upon his back.
Along came a train
Clickety-clack
OOOHH Ooey Gooey!

traditional USA

Catkin

I have a little pussy,
And her coat is silver grey;
She lives in a meadow
And she never runs away.
She always is a pussy,
She'll never be a cat
'Cos she's a pussy willow –
Now what d'you think of that?

Anonymous

Ting-a-ling-bone

Ting-a-ling-bone! Ting-a-ling-bone!
A fire broke out in the little goat's home.
A bucketful of water was fetched by the hen,
To put the fire out if she could, and then
The dogs from the farm-house came as well,
They were bringing a ladder and ringing a bell.
Ting-a-ling-bone! Ting-a-ling-bone!
We'll put out the fire in the little goat's home.

traditional Caribbean

I am a little chestnut

I am a little chestnut brown
Lying on the cold, cold ground.
Someone came and stepped on me,
Now I'm cracked as cracked can be.
I am a nut click, click,
I am a nut click, click,
A nut,
A nut
A nut click, click.

Anonymous

Green cheese

There was an old woman who made green cheese,
By beating up spinach and curds with a spoon;
And when she had done it, with very great ease,
Tossed it up to the sky, and declared 'twas the moon.

Anonymous

The puffin

The puffin is a jolly bird,
It flies above the sea.
It fills its beak
With fish that squeak
And takes them home for tea.

Mark Burgess

Bag of mixed candy

Liquorice slugs and ladybird smarties,
Lemonade wasps and peppermint snails,
Humbugging worms of wriggley's spearmint,
And right at the bottom five fizzy frogs' tails!

Theresa Heine

The bumble-bee

The bumble-bee, the bumble-bee –
He flew to the top of the tulip tree;
He flew to the top, but he could not stop,
For he had to get home to early tea.

The bumble-bee, the bumble-bee –
He flew away from the tulip tree;
But he made a mistake and flew into the lake,
And he never got home early for tea.

Anonymous

The elephant carries a great big trunk

The elephant carries a great big trunk,
But he never packs it with clothes;
It has no lock and it has no key,
But he takes it wherever he goes.

Anonymous

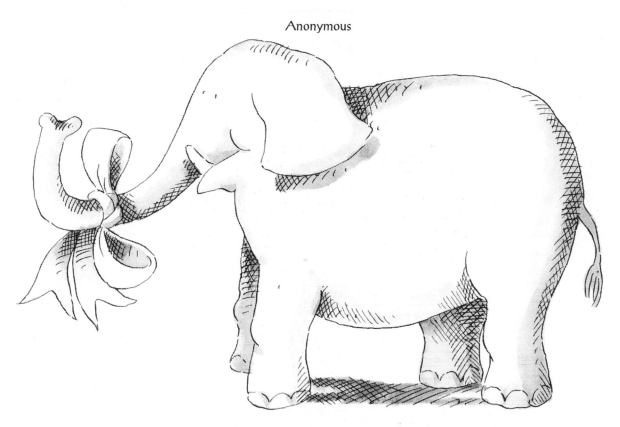

The man in the moon

The man in the moon as he sails through the sky
Is a very remarkable skipper,
But he made a mistake when he tried to take
A drink from the Dipper.
He dipped right out of the Milky Way,
And slowly and carefully filled it,
The Big Bear growled, and the Little Bear howled
And frightened him so he spilled it!

Anonymous

Mary went down to Grandpa's farm

Mary went down to Grandpa's farm;
The billy goat chased her round the barn,
Chased her up the sycamore tree,
And this is the song she sang to me:
'I like coffee, I like tea,
I like the boys and the boys like me.'

Anonymous

Imagine if ...

If the sea was in the sky,
And trees grew underground,
If all the fish had giant teeth,
And all the cows were round;
If birds flew backwards all the time,
And eagles ruled the land;
If bricks poured down instead of rain,
If all the seas were sand;
If everyone had seven heads
And we spoke Double Dutch,
And if the sun came out at night,
We wouldn't like it much.

Anonymous

Mother may I go and bathe?

Mother may I go and bathe?
Yes, my darling daughter.
Hang your clothes up on the tree
But don't go near the water.

Mother may I go and swim?
Yes, my darling daughter.
Fold your clothes up neat and trim
But don't go near the water.

Anonymous

'Twas midnight on the ocean

'Twas midnight on the ocean,
Not a motorcar in sight,
The sun was shining brightly,
For it rained all day that night.
'Twas a summer's day in winter
And snow was raining fast
As a barefoot girl with shoes on
Stood sitting on the grass.

Anonymous

As I was going out one day

As I was going out one day
My head fell off and rolled away.
But when I saw that it was gone,
I picked it up and put it on.

And when I got into the street
A fellow cried, 'Look at your feet!'
I looked at them and sadly said:
'I've left them both asleep in bed!'

Anonymous

The jigsaw bird

I love to see the jigsaw bird
Flying upside down.
It sings a song that sounds all wrong
And wears a dressing-gown.

I love to see the sawjig bird
Flying downside up.
It feeds on chips and concrete mix
And drinks them from a cup.

Mark Burgess

People in the house

Mr Mop has a floppy top.
Mr Broom wants a bit more room.

Mr Brush is in a rush.
Mr Pan goes as quick as he can.

Mr Plate is very late.
Mr Cup is getting up.

Mr Spoon is eating a prune.
Mr Bin is giving a grin.

Mr Towel is making a scowl.
Mr Sheet has got smelly feet.

Charles Thomson

In Regents Park

In Regents Park I met a man
Who did not wear a hat,
But, like a collar, round his neck,
He had a large grey cat.

I stroked its silky fur and asked,
'Where are you going to?'
He said, 'Today is Sunday, so
I'm going to the zoo.'

'My brother's coming with me.'
A man came panting up
And on his head was balancing
A tiny long-haired pup.

I said I'd go along with them,
I buttoned up my coat
And lifted up upon my back
My pure white baby goat.

Barbara Ireson

One fine October morning

One fine October morning
In September, last July,
The moon lay thick upon the ground,
The snow shone in the sky.
The flowers were singing merrily
The birds were in full bloom
I went down to the cellar
To sweep the upstairs room.

Anonymous

Down in the desert

Down in the desert
Where the purple grass dies,
There I saw an old witch
With green and yellow eyes.

traditional USA

As I looked out

As I looked out on Saturday last,
A little fat pig went hurrying past.
Over his shoulders he wore a shawl,
Although it didn't seem cold at all.
I waved at him, but he didn't see,
For he never so much as looked at me.
Once again, when the moon was high,
I saw the little pig hurrying by;
Back he came at a terrible pace,
The moonlight shone on his little pink face,
And he smiled with a smile that was quite content,
But I never knew where that little pig went.

Anonymous

COUNTING RHYMES

Giant's breakfast

I WANT
   ONE sack of sugar on my teaspoon,
   TWO jugs of milk in my tea;
   THREE bags of tea-leaves in the teapot –
   and don't forget to STIR it well for me!

I WANT
   FOUR packs of porridge made with cream now,
   FIVE tins of treacle stirred well in;
   SIX big bananas chopped on top, please –
   I don't want to end up looking THIN!

I WANT
   SEVEN loaves of bread on my plate, please,
   EIGHT jars of jam just for me;
   NINE trays of bacon, egg and sausage –
   I'm not greedy in the morning, as you see!

Judith Nicholls

Five plump peas

Five plump peas in a pea-pod pressed.
Five plump peas in a pea-pod pressed.
One grew, two grew,
And so did all the rest.
They grew and grew
And grew and grew
And grew and never stopped,
Till they grew so fat and round
That the pea-pod – POPPED!

*(Five children could curl up in a line
and grow with the rhyme, finally
leaping into the air when the pod pops.)*

Anonymous

Four seeds

Four seeds in a hole,
Four seeds in a hole –
One for the mouse,
One for the crow;
One to rot and one to grow!

Anonymous

Tik tak toe

Tik, tak, toe,
My first go,
Three jolly farmers
(Show three fingers.)
All in a row;
Stick one up and stick one down,
(Hold one finger up; hold one finger down.)
Stick one in the old man's crown.
(Clench other hand around one finger.)

Anonymous

The bee hive

Here is the bee hive,
(Palms face in and fingers touch.)
Where are the bees?
(Extend hands, palms open.)
Hidden away where nobody sees.
(Clench fists.)
Soon they'll come creeping
(Fingers wriggle.)
Out of the hive,
One, two, three, four, five.
(Show thumb, show thumb and first finger, etc.)

Anonymous

There was a sow

There once was a sow
Who had three piglets,
Three little piglets had she.
And that old sow, she always went
'UMPH',
And the piglets went
'WEE, WEE, WEE.'

Anonymous

Five little pigs

Five little pigs went a-walking,
One little pig fell down,
One little pig, he ran away,
How many got into town?

(The number of pigs can be changed, e.g. start with ten and the children can then supply the answer.)

Anonymous

Good morning Mrs Hen

Chook! chook! chook! chook!
Chook! chook! chook!
– Good morning Mrs Hen.
How many little chicks have you got?
– Madam, I've got ten.
Four of them are yellow,
And four of them are brown,
And two of them are speckled red,
The finest in the town.

Anonymous

Two little birds

Two little birds sat on a stone,
(Clench left fist; hold right hand adjacent to it,
two fingers raised together.)
    Fa, la,la,la,lal, de;
One flew away, and then there was one,
(Waggle one finger and put it down, so one
remains up.)
    Fa, la,la,la,lal, de.

The other flew after and then there was none.
(Waggle the second finger and put it down.)
    Fa, la,la,la,lal, de;
And so the poor stone was left all alone,
(Show the clenched fist of the left hand.)
    Fa, la,la,la,lal, de.

Anonymous

Number one, touch your tongue

Number one, touch your tongue.
Number two, touch your shoe.
Number three, touch your knee.
Number four, touch the floor.
Number five, learn to jive.
Number six, pick up sticks.
Number seven, point to heaven.
Number eight, shut the gate.
Number nine, touch your spine.
Number ten, do it again!

Anonymous

Strawberry pie

Pick a strawberry,
Pop a strawberry
on your tongue;
squeeze it hard
and taste the juice...
pick another one!

One for the basket,
two for the mouth,
three for supper,
four for tea;
five for the dish,
then open wide!
Here's the plumpest
and that's for me!

Pick a strawberry,
pop a strawberry
on your tongue;
squeeze it hard
and taste the juice...
now they've gone!

Judith Nicholls

Me and you

Oh, I've got one head,
And one nose too,
One mouth and one chin
And so have you.
Oh, I've got two eyes,
And two ears too,
Two legs, two arms
And so have you.
Oh, I've got two thumbs
And so have you.

(Children can point to their own
features as they say the rhyme.)

Anonymous

Mosquito one

Mosquito one
mosquito two
mosquito jump
in de old man shoe

traditional Caribbean

Musquito one

Musquito one
musquito two
musquito jump
in the hot callalou

traditional Caribbean

Yat yih saam

Yat yih saam
saam yih yat
Yat yih saam sei ng luhk chat
Yih saam sei
Sei saam yih
Sei ng luhk chat baat gau sahp

traditional Cantonese

One two three
Three two one
One two three four five six seven
Two three four
Four three two
Four five six seven eight nine ten

By'm bye

By'm bye,
By'm bye.
Stars shining,
In the sky.
Number, number one,
Number two, number three,
Good Lawd, by'm bye, by'm bye.
Good Lawd, by'm bye.

traditional USA (Texas)

2,4,6,8

2,4,6,8
Mary's at the cottage gate,
Eating cherries off a
plate.

Anonymous

One, two, three, four

One, two, three, four
Johnny hiding behind de door,
Four, five, six,
Mammy catch him, that stop his tricks.

traditional Caribbean

Ek ne ek be

Ek ne ek be
Be ne ek tran
Tran ne ek char
Char ne ek panch
Panch mara angala
Panch tamara angala

One and one makes two
Two and one makes three
Three and one makes four
Four and one makes five
Five fingers on my hand
And five fingers on your hand.

Panch ne ek chha
Chha ne ek sat
Sat ne ek athh
Athh ne ek nav
Nav ne ek sas
Das mara angala
Das tamara angala

Five and one makes six
Six and one makes seven
Seven and one makes eight
Eight and one makes nine
Nine and one makes ten
Ten fingers on my hands
And ten on yours.

Niru Desai (Gujarati)

(angala = fingers; mara = mine; tamara = yours)

Counting

10
Ten tall vicars sitting down to dine
Blow wind, blow, and that leaves nine.

9
Nine boys and girls swinging on a gate,
Blow wind, blow, and that leaves eight.

8
Eight twinkly stars, shining in the heavens,
Blow wind, blow, and that leaves seven.

7
Seven fat gardeners picking up sticks,
Blow wind, blow, and that leaves six.

6
Six busy bees buzzing by the hive,
Blow wind, blow, and that leaves five.

5
Five spinning spiders above my door,
Blow wind, blow, and that leaves four.

4
Four shivering leaves on the big oak tree,
Blow wind, blow, and that leaves three.

3
Three white storks flying over the zoo,
Blow wind, blow, and that leaves two.

2
Two yellow shirts drying in the sun,
Blow wind, blow, and that leaves one.

1
One little girl with an iced currant bun,
Blow wind, blow, and that leaves none.
0

Ann Marie Linden

One hungry crocodile

One hungry crocodile
Eats two men.
Then he eats the others –
How many to make ten?

One hungry crocodile
Eats three men etc.

*(Use raised fingers to indicate
number of men eaten.)*

Anonymous

One pink sari

One pink sari for a pretty girl,
Two dancing women all in a whirl,
Three charmed cobras rising from a basket,
Four fat rubies, in the Rajah's casket,
Five water carriers straight and tall,
Six wicked vultures sitting on the wall,
Seven fierce tigers hiding in the grass,
Eight elephants rolling in a warm mud bath,
Nine green parrots in the coconut tree,
Ten twinkling stars, a-twinkling at me!

Ann Marie Linden

One for sorrow

One for sorrow, two for joy,
Three for a girl, four for a boy,
Five for silver, six for gold,
Seven for a secret never told.

(Show number of fingers for each phrase.)

Anonymous

Chimney pot

I'm going to build a chimney pot,
I'll build it very high,
I'll build it with my bricks,
And I'll make it touch the sky –
One, two, three, four, five,
Six, seven, eight, nine, ten.
Here comes the wind and here comes the rain.
To knock my chimney down again.

Anonymous

How many people?

How many people live at your house,
At your house, your house?
One – my mother,
Two – my father,
Three – my brother,
Four – my sister.
There must be one more,
Let me see.
Yes, of course,
Number five is...ME!

(Use one finger to represent each person.)

Anonymous

Letters

Every morning at eight o'clock
You can here the mailman's knock.
Up jumps Katy to open the door,
One letter, two letters, three letters,
FOUR.

Anonymous

Ten white snowmen

Ten white snowmen standing in a line,
One toppled over, then there were nine.

Nine white snowmen standing up straight,
One lost his balance, then there were eight.

Eight white snowmen in a snowy heaven,
The wind blew one over, then there were seven.

Seven white snowmen with pipes made of sticks,
One slumped to the ground, then there were six.

Six white snowmen standing by the drive,
One got knocked down, then there were five.

Five white snowmen outside the front door,
An icicle fell on one, then there were four.

Four white snowmen standing by the tree,
One slipped and fell apart, then there were three.

Three white snowmen underneath the yew,
One crumbled overnight, then there were two.

Two white snowmen standing in the sun,
One melted right down, then there was one.

One white snowman standing all alone,
Vanished without a trace, then there was none.

John Foster

Christmas counting

One Christmas tree in a silver pot,
Two gold stars to shine on the top.
Three kings journeying from the East,
Four candles lit on the advent wreath,
Five singers carolling down the lane,
Six presents hidden for Christmas Day,
Seven soft kisses in the mistletoe's light,
Eight reindeer flying swift through the night,
Nine stockings filled on Christmas Eve,
Ten bells welcoming Christ the King!

Theresa Heine

The months of the year

Thirty days hath September,
April, June and November;
All the rest have thirty-one,
Excepting February alone,
And that has twenty-eight days clear
And twenty-nine in each leap year.

Anonymous

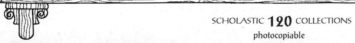

ALL SORTS OF PEOPLE

The old woman

There was an old woman tossed up in a basket,
Seventeen times as high as the moon;
Where she was going I couldn't but ask it,
For in her hand she carried a broom.

Old woman, old woman, old woman, quoth I,
Where are you going to up so high?
To brush the cobwebs out of the sky!
May I go with you? Aye, by-and-by.

Anonymous

Elsi Marley

Elsi Marley is grown so fine,
She won't get up to feed the swine,
But lies in bed till eight or nine,
Lazy Elsi Marley.

Anonymous

Sukey

Sukey, you shall be my wife
And I will tell you why:
I have got a little pig,
And you have got a sty;
I have got a dun cow,
And you can make good cheese;
Sukey, will you marry me?
Say, Yes, if you please.

Anonymous

Charley Barley

Charley Barley, butter and eggs,
Sold his wife for three duck eggs.
When the ducks began to lay,
Charley Barley flew away.

Anonymous

The milkman

Milkman, milkman, where have you been?
In Buttermilk Channel up to my chin.
I spilt my milk, and spoilt my clothes,
And got a long icicle hung from my nose.

Anonymous

Sam, Sam

Sam, Sam, the butcher man,
Washed his face in a frying pan,
Combed his hair with a wagon wheel,
And died with a toothache in his heel.

Anonymous

My maid Mary

My maid Mary,
She minds the dairy,
While I go a-hoeing and mowing each morn;
Merrily run the reel,
And the little spinning wheel,
Whilst I am singing and mowing my corn.

Anonymous

The maid of Scrabble Hill

There was a maid on Scrabble Hill,
And if not dead, she lives there still.
She grew so tall, she reached the sky,
And on the moon, hung clothes to dry.

Anonymous

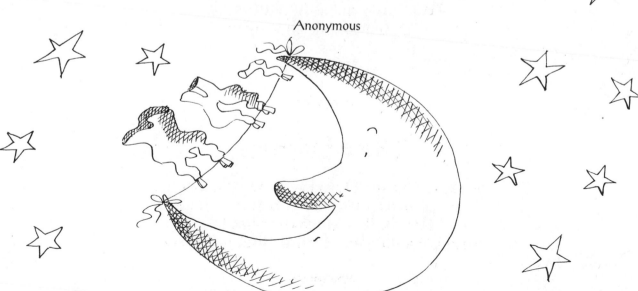

Jacky Jingle

Now what do you think
Of little Jack Jingle?
Before he was married
He used to live single.
But after he married,
To alter his life,
He stopped living single
And lived with his wife.

Anonymous

Tommy Trot

Tommy Trot, a man of law,
Sold his bed and lay upon straw;
Sold the straw and slept on grass,
To buy his wife a looking glass.

Anonymous

Peter

Peter, Peter, pumpkin eater,
Had a wife and couldn't keep her;
He put her in a pumpkin shell
And there he kept her very well.

Anonymous

The bride

Here comes the bride
All dressed in white
White shoes and stockings
And dirty feet inside.

Anonymous

Jemmy Dawson

Brave news is come to town,
Brave news is carried;
Brave news is come to town,
Jemmy Dawson's married.

First he got a porridge-pot,
Then he bought a ladle;
Then he got a wife and child,
And then he bought a cradle.

Anonymous

Eaper Weaper

Eaper Weaper Chimbley Sweeper
Had a wife but couldn't keep her.
Had another, didn't love her
Up the chimbley he did shove her.

Anonymous

Jerry Hall

Jerry Hall,
He is so small,
A rat could eat him,
Hat and all.

Anonymous

Polly Flinders

Little Polly Flinders
Sat among the cinders,
Warming her pretty little toes;
Her mother came and caught her,
And whipped her little daughter
For spoiling her nice new clothes.

Anonymous

Arabella Miller

Little Arabella Miller found a woolly caterpillar.
First it crawled up on her mother,
Then up on her baby brother.
All said, 'Arabella Miller, take away that caterpillar.'

Anonymous

Little boy

Little boy, little boy, where were you born?
Up in the Highlands among the green corn.
Little boy, little boy, where did you sleep?
In the byre with the kye, in a cot with the sheep.

Anonymous

Anna Maria

Anna Maria she sat on the fire;
The fire was too hot, she sat on the pot;
The pot was too round, she sat on the ground;
The ground was too flat, she sat on the cat;
The cat ran away with Maria on her back.

Anonymous

Hector Protector

Hector Protector was dressed all in green;
Hector Protector was sent to the Queen.
The Queen did not like him,
No more did the King;
So Hector Protector was sent back again.

Anonymous

Old Mother Shuttle

Old Mother Shuttle,
Lived in a coal-skuttle
Along with her dog and her cat;
What they ate I can't tell,
But 'tis known very well
That not one of the party was fat.

Old Mother Shuttle
Scoured out her coal-skuttle,
And washed both her dog and her cat;
The cat scratched her nose,
So they came to hard blows,
And who was the gainer by that?

Anonymous

Jeremiah Obadiah

Jeremiah Obadiah, puff, puff, puff.
When he gives his messages he snuffs, snuffs, snuffs,
When he goes to school by day he roars, roars, roars,
When he goes to bed at night he snores, snores, snores,
When he goes to Christmas treat he eats plum duff,
Jeremiah Obadiah, puff, puff, puff.

Anonymous

Queen Caroline

Queen, Queen Caroline,
Washed her hair in turpentine,
Turpentine to make it shine,
Queen, Queen Caroline.

Anonymous

Yankee Doodle

Yankee Doodle came to town,
Riding on a pony;
He stuck a feather in his cap
And called it macaroni.

Anonymous

Granfa' Grig

Granfa' Grig kept a pig,
In a field of clover;
Piggle died, Granfa' cried,
All the fun was over.

Anonymous

Lucy and Kitty

Lucy Locket lost her pocket,
Kitty Fisher found it;
Not a penny was there in it,
Only a ribbon round it.

Anonymous

The farmer of Leeds

There was a young farmer of Leeds,
Who swallowed six packets of seeds.
It soon came to pass
He was covered with grass,
And he couldn't sit down for the weeds.

Anonymous

Miss MacKay

Alas! alas! poor Miss MacKay!
Her knives and forks have run away;
And when the cups and spoons will go,
Poor Miss MacKay, she does not know.

Anonymous

Little Miss Lily

Little Miss Lily
You're dreadfully silly
To wear such a very long skirt.
If you take my advice,
You would hold it up nice,
And not let it trail in the dirt.

Anonymous

Terence McDiddler

Terence McDiddler,
The three-stringed fiddler,
Can charm if you please,
The fish from the seas.

Anonymous

Herbert the Hobo

Herbert the Hobo, he hopped on a train
And he lived in a boxcar from Georgia to Maine!
They didn't collect and he didn't pay rent.
He followed the engine wherever it went!

Anonymous

Joe Jenkins

J was Joe Jenkins
Who played upon the fiddle;
He began to play it twenty times,
But left off in the middle.

Anonymous

Chokri anay bakri

Ek hati chokri
Anay pali bakri.

Chokri ghaie farva
Bakri ghaie charva.

Farine avi chokri
Ditthi nahi bakri.

Chokri laagi rowa,
ay...ay...ay.
Avi pahochi bakri
Karti ba...ba...ba.
traditional Gujarati

The girl and her goat

There was a girl
Who had a pet goat.

The girl went out visiting
The goat went grazing.

When the girl returned
The goat was gone.

The girl began to cry,
boo...boo...boo.
Along came the goat crying
ba...ba...ba.

Ram nagar sae Raja aye

Ram nagar sae Raja aye
Roop nagar sae Rani
Rani roti sake rahi hai
Raja bharate pani.
traditional Hindi

The king has come from Ram nagar
The queen is from Roop nagar
The queen is making bread
The king is getting water.

The man in the moon

The man in the moon
Came down too soon,
And asked the way to Norwich;
He went by south,
And burnt his mouth
With supping cold plum porridge.

Anonymous

Bedtime

The man in the moon looked out of the moon,
Looked out of the moon and said,
' 'Tis time for all the children on earth
To think about getting to bed.'

Anonymous

Pretty maid

Pretty maid, pretty maid,
Where have you been?
Gathering roses
To give to the queen.
Pretty maid, pretty maid,
What gave she you?
She gave me a diamond,
As big as my shoe.

Anonymous

Balloon seller

Buy a balloon,
I have heart ones and round ones,
pink ones and blue ones,
and merry-go-round ones,
balloons that are diamond shaped,
triangles too,
they dance with the clouds
in soft springtime blue.

Theresa Heine

Sammy Soapsuds

When little Sammy Soapsuds
went out to take a ride,
on looking over London Bridge
he fell into the tide.

His parents never having taught
their little Sam to swim,
the tide soon got the better
and made an end of him.

Anonymous

Little Miss Pidget

Little Miss Pidget
is all of a fidget:
she tells me to tie up my shoes.
She puts on my plate
all the things that I hate,
and never allows me to choose.

She asks, 'Are you CLEAN?
Where on earth have you been?
Your hands are both covered with dirt.
There's blood on your knee,
and it's simple to see
you have torn a great hole in your shirt!'

Little Miss Pidget
is shrill as a midget.
She fusses and squeaks like a mouse.
She says that a sweet
is a TERRIBLE treat
and there mustn't be one in the house.

She cries, 'I declare!
There are knots in your hair –
you must cut it and comb it TODAY!
When she visits, I wish
with a swirl and a swish
that a tempest
      would
        blow
          her
            away!
              Per-oof!
                That a tempest
                  would blow her
                    away...

Jean Kenward

Gregory Griggs

Gregory Griggs, Gregory Griggs,
Had twenty seven different wigs.
He wore them up, he wore them down,
To please the people of the town:
He wore them east, he wore them west,
But he could never tell which he loved the best.

Anonymous

Old Hank

For a lark,
For a prank,
Old Hank
Walked a plank.
These bubbles mark
O
  O
O
  O
O
Where Hank sank.

Anonymous

Old John Muddlecombe

Old John Muddlecombe
Lost his cap.
He couldn't find it anywhere,
Poor old chap.

He walked down the street,
And everybody said:
'Silly John Muddlecombe,
You've got it on your head!'

Anonymous

Lollipop lady

Lollipop lady,
lollipop lady,
wave your magic stick
and make the traffic
stop a while
so we can cross the street.

Trucks and cars
rushing past
have no time for little feet.
They hate to wait
especially when late
but we'll be late too
except for you.

So lollipop lady,
lollipop lady,
in the middle of the street
wave your magic stick
and make the traffic
give way to little feet.

John Agard

Some people

Some people are merry
some people are cross,
some people are down
in the dumps.

Some people say NO
when you offer them sweets.
Some people like sugar
in lumps.

Some people are pretty
some people are plain,
some people grow hair
on their head...

And some go about
with their clothes inside out...
SOME PEOPLE wear bonnets
in bed.
    Bang! Bang!
        Some people
            wear bonnets
                in bed.

Jean Kenward

High on the wall

High on the wall
Where the pennywort grows
Polly Penwarden
Is painting her toes.

One is purple
And two are red
And two are the colour
Of her golden head.

One is blue
And two are green
And the others are the colours
They've always been.

Charles Causley

PLAYTIME

Seaside

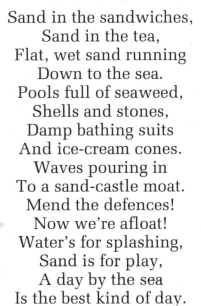

Sand in the sandwiches,
Sand in the tea,
Flat, wet sand running
Down to the sea.
Pools full of seaweed,
Shells and stones,
Damp bathing suits
And ice-cream cones.
Waves pouring in
To a sand-castle moat.
Mend the defences!
Now we're afloat!
Water's for splashing,
Sand is for play,
A day by the sea
Is the best kind of day.

Shirley Hughes

Twist about

Twist about, and turn about,
Jump Jimmy Crow,
Every time I wheel about
I do just so.

Anonymous

Craney crow

Chickamy, chickamy, craney crow,
I went to the well to wash my toe.
When I got back, my chickens were gone.
What time is it, Old Witch?
One o'clock, two o'clock, three ...

Anonymous

Here we go dancing

Here we go dancing, jingo-ring,
Jingo-ring, jingo-ring,
Here we go dancing, jingo-ring,
About the merry-ma-tanzie.

Twice about and then we fall,
Then we fall, then we fall,
Twice about and then we fall,
About the merry-ma-tanzie.

Anonymous

Annie, Annie

Annie, Annie
Climbing trees,
Scrapes her elbows,
Skins her knees,
Scuffs her shoes
And snags her hair –
What's Annie doing
Way up there?

Annie, Annie
Says it's fun
Climbing closer
To the sun,
Far up where
It's grand to be
As high as high
And swinging free.

Beverly McLoughland

One-amy, uery, hickory, seven

One-amy, uery, hickory, seven,
Hallibone, crackabone, ten and eleven,
Peep-O, it must be done,
Twiggle, twaggle, twenty-one.

traditional USA

Eny, meny, mony, my

Eny, meny, mony, my,
Tusca, leina, bona stry,
Kay, bell, broken well,
We, wo, wack.

Anonymous

Onery, uery, ickery, see

Onery, uery, ickery, see,
Huckabone, crackabone, tillibonee,
Ram, pang, muski dan,
Striddledum, straddledum, twenty-one.

traditional USA

Ūkkur dūkkur bumba bo

(Turn taking song)

Ūkkur dūkkur bumba bo
Ussi nubbay poora saw
Saw gulota titur mota
Chul mudari paisa khota
traditional Punjabi

Key to pronunciation:
a=at ee=feet oa=coat ū=put
aa=car i=pin oo=moon u=but
ay=pay ia=familiar ow=cow th=thin
e=bet o=got oy=boy (n)=nasal sound

*(This guide may be helpful in the
other Punjabi poems.)*

━━━━━━

Baak bakum paira

Baak bakum paira
Matay die taira
Bow shazbe kalki
Chorrbe shonar palki
traditional Bengali

Coo pigeon
Bring the wedding crown
The bride marries tomorrow
She will go away on a golden cart.

*(Possible actions: flap arms like a bird, put on a crown,
palms together, move hands round in a circle,
roll hands round each other.)*

Draw a bucket of water

Draw a bucket of water
For my lady's daughter.
One in a rush,
Two in a rush,
Here we go round the mulberry bush.
traditional USA

Little Sally Water

Little Sally Water sprinkle in your saucer;
Rise Sally rise an' wipe your weeping eyes.
Sally turn to the east,
Sally turn to the west,
Sally turn to the one you like the best.
traditional Jamaican

Charley over the water

Charley over the water,
Charley over the sea,
Charley catch a blackbird,
Can't catch me!
traditional USA

Abna Babna

Abna Babna
Lady-Snee
Ocean potion
Sugar and tea
Potato roast
And English toast
O-U-T and out goes she.
traditional Caribbean

Two, four, six, eight

Two, four, six, eight,
Jenny saw a rattlesnake,
Eating cake by the lake,
Two, four, six, eight.

Anonymous

As I was walking round the lake

As I was walking round the lake
I met a little rattlesnake
I gave him so much jelly cake
It made his little belly ache
One, two, three
And out goes she.

Anonymous

Here comes a blue-bird

Here comes a blue-bird through the window,
Here comes a blue-bird through the window,
Here comes a blue-bird through the window,
High dum diddle dum day.

Take a little dance and a hop-i'-the-corner,
Take a little dance and a hop-i'-the-corner,
Take a little dance and a hop-i'-the-corner,
High dum diddle dum day.

traditional USA

Juba this and Juba that

Juba this and Juba that,
Juba killed the yellow cat,
Juba up and Juba down,
Juba running all around.

Juba this and Juba that,
Juba killed the yellow cat,
Juba up and Juba down,
Juba clapping all around.

(Sing through 4 times:
1st time repeat verse slowly and loudly.
2nd time repeat verse a little slower, a little
softer, clapping hands in rhythm.
3rd time repeat verse a little faster and softer
still, slap both hands on knees, then clap
hands together in rhythm.
4th time repeat verse very fast and very soft.
At same time slap hands on knees, clap
hands together, clap hands on both cheeks,
clap hands together again in rhythm.)

Anonymous

My eyes can see

My eyes can see.
(Make spectacles with hands.)
My mouth can talk.
(Bring index finger down on thumb repeatedly.)
My ears can hear.
(Cup hand and put behind ear.)
My feet can walk.
(Palms down, wriggle 2nd and 3rd fingers.)
My nose can smell.
(Touch nose with fingertip.)
My teeth can bite.
(Palms together, move fingertips together and back.)
My eyelids can flutter.
(Hold hands close to eyes, move fingers up and down.)
My hands can write.
(Pretend to hold pencil and write.)

Anonymous

Throw your nets

Throw, throw, throw your nets,
(Pretend to throw using both arms.)
Out into the sea,
Pull them in,
Pull them in,
(Pull arms slowly to body.)
And give your fish to me!
(Point to self.)

Anonymous

Clap your hands

Clap your hands, clap your hands,
Clap them just like me.

Touch your shoulders, touch your shoulders,
Touch them just like me.

Tap your knees, tap your knees,
Tap them just like me.

Shake your head, shake your head,
Shake it just like me.

Clap your hands, clap your hands,
Now let them quiet be.

Anonymous

Hands up

Hands up to the ceiling
Hands touch the floor,
Reach up again,
Let's do some more.
Now touch your head,
Then touch your knee,
Then touch your shoulder,
Just like me.
Hands up to the ceiling,
Hands touch the floor.
That's all for now, goodbye –
There isn't any more.

Anonymous

Squirting rainbows

Bare legs,
Bare toes,
Paddling pool,
Garden hose.
Daisies sprinkled
In the grass,
Dandelions
Bold as brass.
Squirting rainbows,
Sunbeam flashes,
Backyards full
Of shrieks and splashes!

Shirley Hughes

Ten tom-toms

Ten tom-toms,
Timpany, too,
Ten tall tubas
And an old kazoo.

Ten trombones –
Give them a hand!
The sitting-standing-marching-running
Big Brass Band.

Anonymous

Who's in there?

Who's in the castle
high on the hill?
A great greedy giantess
eating her fill.

Who's in that cottage
there through the trees?
A wily old wizard
with knobbly knees.

Who's in that cavern,
so dark and so scary?
A mischievous monster.
He's big and he's hairy.

Who's in the clouds
flying higher and higher?
A dangerous dragon
breathing out fire.

Who's in that tree stump
made into a home?
He's ever so tiny.
He must be a gnome.

Who's in the tower
so high in the air?
A beautiful princess
who lets down her hair.

Who is it croaking
inside that old log?
He's wearing a crown.
It's a fairytale frog.

Who is that singing
behind the wet rocks?
Look! It's a mermaid
combing her locks.

Who's in the kitchen
making my tea?
It's Mummy and Daddy.
They're waiting for *me*.

Tony Mitton

Towers

One brick, two brick,
Three brick, four.
Whoops go the bricks
All over the floor.

I'm trying to build
A tall brick tower.
Down come the bricks
In a tumbling shower.

Balance one, perch one...
A trembling stack.
Smash, bang, clatter,
Smackety crack.

Here's another tower.
Watch it sway.
Here comes a hand
To knock it away.

Tony Mitton

So, you want to be a wizard?

So, you want to be a wizard?
Well, you'll need a pointed hat
with golden stars and silver moon
and perched on top...a bat.

So you want to be a wizard?
Well, you'll need Ye book of Spells,
and rotten eggs and herring heads
to make some ghastly smells.

So you want to be a wizard?
Well, you'll need some pickled brains,
a wand, a cloak, and one dead rat.
And, yes, slime from the drains.

You *still* want to be a wizard?

Wes Magee

Late on a dark and stormy night

Late on a dark and stormy night,
Three witches stirred with all their might.
Two little ghosts said, 'How d'ye do?'
The wizard went tiptoe, tiptoe...
BOOOOOO!

Anonymous

Jumping song

Jump – jump higher
jump – jump high!
Go and bring a star down
from the night sky!

Go and fill a basket
with little ones and light,
big stars and small stars
and stars out of sight!

Jump – jump higher –
jump up to the moon –
gather what you find there,
and come down soon!

Jean Kenward

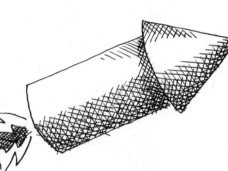

Playtime

Let's fly to the Moon to play today
In spacesuits the colour of lead,
On moonbeams we'll ride, in our spaceship we'll hide,
But I want to come home to my bed.

Let's shoot to the stars to play today,
We'll go in a rocket instead,
We'll sparkle today and shine while we play,
And then I'll come home to my bed.

Let's go on a rainbow to play today
'Midst yellow and orange and red,
We'll have lots of fun and play in the sun,
But I want to come home to my bed.

Penelope Browning

Hippetty hop to the candy shop

Hippetty hop to the candy shop
To buy a stick of candy.
One for you and one for me,
And one for sister Sandy.

Anonymous

Hickety, bickety, pease, scone

Hickety, bickety, pease, scone,
Where shall this poor Scotsman gang?
Will he gang east, or will he gang west,
Or will he gang to the crow's nest?

traditional Scottish

Lakri ki kaati

Lakri ki kaati, kaati pay ghora
Ghohray ki dum pay jo mara hathora
Dawra dawra, dawra ghora.
Dum daba kay dawra.

la la la la la la la
la la la la la la la

traditional Hindi

Rocking horse on his wooden frame,
If you smack him on his tail,
he'll run like anything.

TRANSPORT AND MACHINES

Looping the loop

Zooperty zooperty zoop,
the aeroplane's looping the loop.
It's zooming up,
it's zooming down,
it's zooming high
above the town.

Charles Thomson

Aeroplanes, aeroplanes

Aeroplanes, aeroplanes, look where they fly.
Aeroplanes, aeroplanes, high in the sky.
Their engines are noisy, they make a loud hum.
Now I'm a plane. Look out! Here I come!

Barbara Ireson

Taking off

The aeroplane taxis down the field
And heads into the breeze,
It lifts its wheels above the ground,
It skims above the trees,
It rises high and higher
Away toward the sun,
It's just a speck against the sky
– And now it's gone!

Anonymous

Transport

Some people come to school by bus.
Some people come by train.
Some people come in private car –
but I run down the lane!

Some people bicycle to school.
Some people drive a van –
I like to skip from door to door...
Catch me, if you can!

Jean Kenward

Driving Grandad

Grandad can't stand aeroplanes
or modern cars, electric trains
or motorbikes. He doesn't mind a boat.
When Daddy takes him out, you know
He makes him drive the car so slow
The milkman overtakes us on his float.

Jean Willis

Early in the morning

Come down to the station early in the morning,
See all the railway trains standing in a row.
See all the drivers starting up the engines,
Clickety click and clackety clack,
Off they go!

Come down to the garage early in the morning,
See all the buses standing in a row.
See all the drivers starting up the engines,
Rumble, rumble, rumble, rumble,
Off they go!

Come down to the seaside early in the morning,
See all the motor-boats floating in a row.
See all the drivers starting up the engines,
Splishing, splishing, sploshing, sploshing,
Off they go!

Come down to the airport early in the morning,
See all the aeroplanes standing in a row.
See all the pilots starting up the engines,
Whirring, whirring, whirring, whirring,
Off they go!

Anonymous

Alu, bhindi, kakri, baingan

Alu, bhindi, kakri, baingan
Bhari hui hai station wagon
Essae dekha do hari jhandi
Pahucha de ye sabzi mandi.
traditional Hindi

With potato, okra, pumpkin and aubergine
Full to the brim goes the station wagon
As soon as it sees the two green flags
It will unload at the market place.

Can I come along?

Train, train,
rattling along,
where are you going to?
Can I come along?

From station to station,
from coast to coast,
where do you like going
the most?

Train, train,
thundering along,
where are you going to?
Can I come along?

From sunrise to sunset,
from east to west,
where do you like going
the best?

Train, train,
whistling along –
where are you going?
Where have you gone?

Tony Bradman

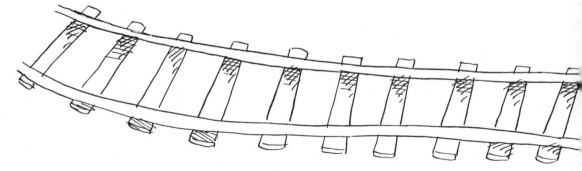

Train ride

Steam train
slides over tracks
through silent countryside;
a dark snake stalking through tall grass,
hissing.

Judith Nicholls

The Underground Snake

What is that rumbling
under the ground?
What is that rushing
and shuddering sound?

Feel the world tremble.
Feel the earth quake.
It must be the race
of the Underground Snake.

With its sinuous length
in a snakeskin of steel
it slips through the ways
of the earth like an eel.

But as it emerges
from out of its cave
I won't run away
and I'll try to be brave.

For I know it's quite tame
and will take you and me
through the dark to our homes,
to our telly and tea.

Tony Mitton

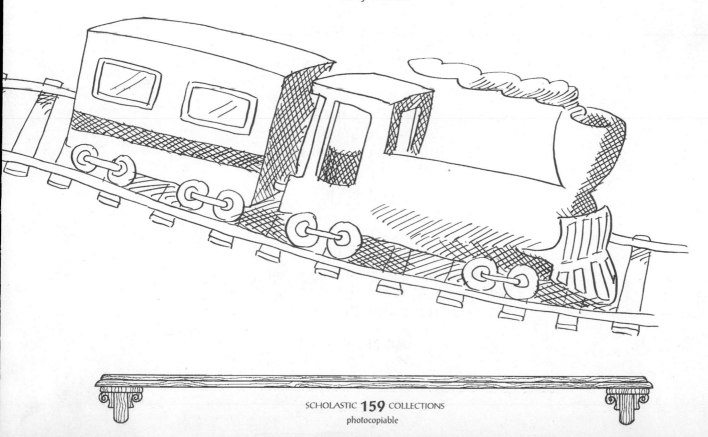

Windscreen wiper

Flicker flicker flack!
Flicker flicker flack!
The wiper on the car goes
Flicker flicker flack,
The rain falls flick!
The rain falls flack!
And the wiper on the car goes
Flicker, flicker, flack!
Flick!
Flack!

S. K. Vickery

The little red bus

Oh, the little red bus goes
Ting ting ting,
Ting ting ting, ting ting ting,
The little red bus goes
Ting ting ting,
Early in the morning.

Oh, the little blue train goes
Chuff chuff chuff,
Chuff chuff chuff, chuff chuff chuff,
The little blue train goes
Chuff chuff chuff,
Early in the morning.

Oh, the little green scooter goes
Pop pop pop,
Pop pop pop, pop pop pop,
The little green scooter goes
Pop pop pop,
Early in the morning.

Oh, the big jet plane goes
Whee...
Whee... whee...,
The big jet plane goes
Whee...,
Early in the morning.

Michael John

The double-decker bus

We like riding on the double-decker bus.
Up on the top-deck that's the place for us!

In the front seat with the driver down below,
We give the orders, tell him where to go.

Tell him when to speed up, when to slow down.
We drive the double-decker right through town.

We drive it up the hill and park by the gate.
We make sure that the bus is never late.

We like riding on the double-decker bus.
The front seat on the top deck –
That's the place for us!

John Foster

I love to row

I love to row in my big blue boat,
My big blue boat, my big blue boat;
I love to row in my big blue boat,
Out on the deep blue sea.

The big blue boat has two red sails,
Two red sails, two red sails;
My big blue boat has two red sails,
And oars for you and me.

So come and row in my big blue boat,
My big blue boat, my big blue boat;
So come and row in my big blue boat,
Out on the deep blue sea.

Anonymous

The ferry

'Ferry me across the water,
Do, boatman, do.'
'If you've a penny in your purse
I'll ferry you.'

'I have a penny in my pocket
And my eyes are blue;
So ferry me across the water,
Do, boatman, do.'

'Step into my ferry-boat
Be they black or blue
And for the penny in your purse
I'll ferry you.'

Christina Rossetti

Scooter

Who comes speeding down the street?
– Two round wheels,
And two small feet,
And two tight hands to steer the way?
It's me!
And here I come!
Hooray!

Lydia Pender

Eating an icicle

Eating an icicle, riding my bicycle,
Rolling along in the wind, rain and snow;
Chewing so happily, pedalling snappily
Backward and forward through gears high and low.
Icicle, bicycle, sometimes a tricycle,
Snappily, happily onward I go.

Nancy Chambers

Journey into space

We went on a journey
A journey, a journey.
We went in a rocket
Jaswinder and me.
We went past the moon
And we went past the planets.
We sailed into Sunspace,
Jaswinder and me.
We landed at daybreak,
At daybreak, at daybreak
We landed in secret,
Jaswinder and me.
Then the aliens found us
And danced all around us
And made plans to crown us
Jaswinder and me.
But we climbed in our rocket,
Our rocket, our rocket,
And zoomed back to earth,
Just in time for our tea.

Irene Yates

Humpty Dumpty went to the moon

Humpty Dumpty went to the moon
on a supersonic spoon
He took some porridge and a tent
but when he landed
the spoon got bent.
Humpty said he didn't care
and for all I know
he's still up there.

Michael Rosen

Immediate despatch

Polish up the spaceship,
Shine, shine, shine,
Fill up the fuel tanks
In time, time, time,
Switch on the motor
And close down the hatch.
Moonship Apollo
Immediate despatch.

Shooting into outer space
Zoom, zoom, zoom,
Circling round and round the earth
There's room, room, room,
Watch every lever
And check every clock.
Moonship Apollo
Is ready to dock.

Jean Gilbert

My telescope

I bought myself a telescope
To look into the sky,
To see the solar system
And the comets whizzing by.

I search the sky for planets,
For satellites and stars,
And now I've got a telescope
They don't seem very far.

It's brought them very close to me,
It's made the stars my friends...
Except of course when I make a mistake
And look through the wrong end!

Tony Bradman

Night rider

I have a flying horse named Ned,
And often when I'm put to bed
I wait till all is quiet, and then
I put my track-suit on again.
Out of the window, off we go.
We soar up high, we swoop down low,
We speed across the velvet sky,
A Jumbo Jet goes roaring by.
A spacecraft slips between the stars,
Brimful of green-skinned men from Mars.
We hope maybe that one day soon
We'll get as far as Old Man Moon.
But we must hurry home, you see,
In case my family misses me.

Margaret McCarthy

It's raining

It's raining, it's hailing,
The stars give no light.
My little horse must travel
This dark and stormy night.

Go put him in the stable
And give him some hay;
Come sit in the cottage
As long as you can stay.

My horse isn't hungry,
He won't eat your hay,
And I must be riding
Until it is day.

Anonymous

Chal mera ghora

Chal mera ghora tick tick tick
chal mera ghora tick tick tick
Rhukanay khatum namna lana
Chalana tera kam
Chal mera ghora tick tick tick.

traditional Hindi

Run my horse
Run my horse
Don't you think of stopping
Your job is to gallop
Run my horse.

There's a hole in my pants

There's a hole in my pants.
It's our washing machine.
It's eating our clothes,
Not washing them clean.

As it churns round and round,
It snorts and it snickers,
Chewing holes in Dad's shirts
And ripping Mum's knickers.

It's swallowed a sock.
We can't open the door.
It's bubbling out soap suds
All over the floor.

There's a monster that lives
In our washing machine.
It's eating our clothes,
Not washing them clean.

John Foster

Hair-drier

My mum's hair-drier
buzzes like a bee
Looks like a ray gun
when she points it at me

'Into the bath now,
Let's shampoo that hair,
then out for a rub down
and a blow of hot air.'

It prickles my head
and tingles my ears
It tickles my neck
as it zooms and it whirrs

It whizzes and whooshes
and buzzes at me
It sounds much more like
a bad-tempered bee!

Maggie Holmes

The telly monster

There's a monster in our telly.
He's in there every night.
I hear his voice
And see his eyes,
He's such a fearful sight.

I think I'll get
A great big stick
And bop him on the head.
A fearful telly monster
Can't hurt you
If he's DEAD!

Gordon Winch

Here comes the robot

Here comes the robot
Bzz Bzz, VROOM!
someone's switched it on
and it's running round the room

Here comes the robot
Bzz Bzz, CRASH!
It's sitting on the table
eating sausages and mash

Here comes the robot
Bzz Bzz, SPLOSH!
It's made the bathroom floor all wet
trying to have a wash

Here comes the robot
Bzz Bzz, BLEEP!
It's sitting in front of the telly
and fallen fast asleep.

Michael Rosen

New wheelchair

When John is in his new wheelchair
everybody stops to stare.
It's got a motor with extra power –
it goes a hundred miles an hour.

Charles Thomson

Road sweeper machine

Sweeper, sweeper, clean-road-keeper,
swept my sister – wouldn't keep her!
Spat her from the suction hose
wearing only underclothes.

Gina Douthwaite

To the fair

When Dad and I went to the fair
we tried out all of the rides,
we dodged about on the dodgems
and whizzed down the astro slide.
Then we rode the roller coaster
and it gave us quite a scare:
'One thing is certain,' Dad said,
'I'm not going back on there!'

Brian Moses

SEASONS

Wind

The wind blows the windmill,
the wind blows me.
Where does the wind go?
Can you see?

The wind blows feathers,
the wind blows fluff,
whirling around
all kinds of stuff:

Paper, flags,
and leaves, and hair –
what do they do
when the wind's not there?

The wind blows the sea
with splosh and splash;
the wind blows the window –
bang and crash!

The wind blows around
like a roundabout.
Hold on tightly
or he'll blow you out!

Jean Kenward

The wind has such a rainy sound

The wind has such a rainy sound
    Moaning through the town,
The sea has such a windy sound –
    Will the ships go down?

The apples in the orchard
    Tumble from their tree –
Oh, will the ships go down, go down,
    In the windy sea?

Christina Rossetti

I hear thunder

I hear thunder, I hear thunder
(Stamp feet on floor.)
Hark, don't you, hark, don't you?
(Put hand to ear.)
Pitter-patter raindrops,
(Move hand down slowly, waggling fingers.)
Pitter-patter raindrops,
I'm wet through –
(Shake body.)
You are too.
(Point to someone else.)

Anonymous

Plippetty, clippetty

The rain comes pittering pattering down,
    Plippetty, plippetty, plop.
The farmer drives his horse to town,
    Clippetty, clippetty clop.
The rain comes pattering,
Horse goes clattering,
    Clippetty, clippetty, clop.

Anonymous

The storm

Listen can you hear the rain?
See the lightning flash.
Now it's thundering again.
Can you hear the crash?

Anonymous

Winter walk

Walking home from Granny's
On a dark and snowy night.
Everything looks ghostly
In the shadowy street light.

All is still and quiet.
No footsteps can be heard,
Except the crunch beneath us.
Too cold to say a word.

Wendy Larmont

Storm

The clouds are dark
above my house.
The sky is full of rain.
There's thunder deeply rumbling
and droplets on the pane.

So I shall stay inside my house
because it's dry and warm.
I'll stand beside the window
and watch the growing storm.

Tony Mitton

Hands are cold

Hands are cold
and feet are cold;
icy winds are blowing.
Rub your hands
and stamp your feet
and soon they will be glowing.

Anonymous

Evening red

Evening red and morning grey,
Send the traveller on his way;
Evening grey and morning red
Bring the rain upon his head.

Anonymous

Rain

Rain on the green grass,
    And rain on the tree,
And rain on the house top
    But not on me.

Anonymous

Rain and snow

This is the way the rain drops
down
    down
        down,
pattering on the open fields
    spluttering in the town
scattering over the lily pool
    circles and steeples tall...
This is the way the rain drops —
    raindrops
        fall.

This is the way the snow drifts
low
    low
        low,
flying upon the roof tops
    fluttering far below
feathering over the flower beds
    whitening green and brown...
This is the way the snow drifts —
    snow drifts
        down.

Jean Kenward

Rain, rain, go away

Rain, rain, go away,
Come again another day.
Little Johnny wants to play.

Anonymous

Sun and rain

The rain makes the ground wet,
The sun makes the ground dry,
Sun and rain help the crops
To grow tall and high.

Anonymous

Rain rhymes

The rain is falling on the ground.
It makes a lovely liquid sound.
A dripping splishing sploshing splashing.
In the wind, a luscious lashing.
When it drops, a peaceful plashing.
Cars are swooshing, people dashing,
children stamping: puddle bashing.
Roofs are sheened and slates are flashing.
Slantwise lines of rain are slashing.
Sleek and shiny rain is smashing.

Tony Mitton

Spring sunshine

It's nice to see the sun again,
It makes the whole world shine,
It brings the buds to flower again
And warms your face and mine.

Theresa Heine

Weather

Weather comes and weather goes,
Autumn winds and winter snows.

Sometimes cold and sometimes hot,
Sometimes raining, sometimes not.

Summer sun and springtime green,
The brightest rainbow ever seen.

No matter what we do or say,
We have weather every day.

Theresa Heine

Seasons turn

Spring is freshness,
leafy green,
soft pale buds
where snow has been.

Summer glows,
the sun is hot,
can you find
a shady spot?

Autumn's wild,
it stamps and roars,
blows the leaves
and bangs the doors.

Winter's chilly
snow and frost,
better find
the gloves you lost.

Theresa Heine

Buy sweet daffodils

Buy sweet daffodils,
Tulips from Amsterdam,
Narcissus white and gold
Spring flowers to be sold.

Anonymous

Daffodillies yellow

Daffodillies yellow
Daffodillies gay
To put on the table
On Easter day.

Anonymous

Mayday

Round and round the maypole
Merrily we go
Tripping tripping lightly
Singing as we go.

Anonymous

On Mayday we dance

On Mayday we dance,
On Mayday we sing,
For this is the day
We welcome the spring.

Anonymous

It's Pancake Day

It's Pancake Day!
It's Pancake Day!
Hurry home to tea!
There'll be pancakes for you!
There'll be pancakes for me!

Dad's cooking pancakes
In the frying pan,
Turning them by tossing them
As high as he can.

It's Pancake Day!
It's Pancake Day!
Sit down for your tea.
There's pancakes for you!
There's pancakes for me!

Dad's made some pancakes,
Crisp and golden brown,
Sprinkle them with sugar
And gobble them down!

John Foster

The Festival of [
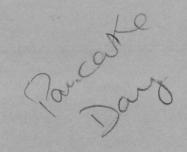

Enjoy the Festival of H[
When many bonfires are a[
Join the dancing and the si[
For the time of harvest is now[

See the children with coloured[
Spraying grown-ups till they're red[
Hear the shrill horns and clangin[
We must all join in this noisy [

Janet Greenyer

'Id-al-Fitr

*(a skipping chant for
the end of Ramadan)*

Ramadan
Ramadan
New Moon
New Moon
*Break the fast,
Break the fast!*

Samora, pakora,
Pamosa, samosa,
Tappati, chappati,
Sambal, poppadom...
NOW!

Judith Nicholls

Eid

We paint our hands with flowers
We wear new clothes and shoes.
We give sweets to our family
And find out all the news.

Now Ramadan is over
And we can end our fast.
Let's have a celebration.
Eid is here at last.

Wendy Larmont

Down in the orchard

Down in the orchard
It's harvest time
And up the tall ladders
The fruit pickers climb.

Among the green branches
That sway overhead
The apples are hanging
All rosy and red.

Just ripe for picking
All juicy and sweet
So pretty to look at
And tasty to eat.

Anonymous

August heat

In August, when the days are hot,
I like to find a shady spot,
And hardly move a single bit –
And sit –
    And sit –
        And sit –
           And sit!

Anonymous

Come October

Come October
spiders
striped as humbugs
spin their linings.

Come October
berries
strung in clusters
bead the hedgerows.

Come October
colours
traffic-light trees
signal winter.

Come October
conkers
polished bombshells
wink and tumble.

Come October
dry leaves
cornflake carpets
lie in deep drifts.

Come October
bonfires
smoky dragons
lick the night sky.

Sue Cowling

Feasts

Apples heaped on market barrows,
Juicy plums and stripy marrows.
Grains of barley,
Carefully stored,
Feasts of berries,
Nuts to hoard,
And ripe pumpkins, yellow and green,
To light with candles at Hallowe'en.

Shirley Hughes

Fireworks!

(A chant for two groups of voices)

Squibs and sparklers
Squibs and sparklers
Golden showers
Golden showers
Shooting stars and Catherine wheels
Shooting stars and Catherine wheels
Fiery flowers
Fiery flowers
Racing rockets
Racing rockets
Whirling windmills
Whirling windmills
Flashing fountains
Flashing fountains
Blazing mountains
Blazing mountains
Light the paper...
Watch them whizzing
Watch them whizzing
Watch them whizzing,
B A N G !

Judith Nicholls

November the fifth

Whizzing, flashing, whirling,
Silver, red and gold.
Catherine wheels and rockets,
Sparklers bright to hold.

Burst of showering fireworks
Fizzing in the sky.
Smoky, crackling bonfire,
On top, there's the guy.

Holding baked potatoes
From the fire so red.
Now the display's over.
Safely home to bed.

Wendy Larmont

Guy Fawkes night

I look up to the dark night sky,
I hear the rockets scream,
Then a million coloured stars fall down,
It's really like a dream.

I watch the blazing bonfire,
'Till smoke gets in my eyes,
The Catherine wheels begin to spin,
'There's a banger!' someone cries.

And when the fireworks finish,
We have sausages to eat,
They're pushed inside those soft white rolls,
It really is a treat.

Janet Greenyer

Diwali morning

There's a rangoli pattern in front of our door,
'Diwali Mubarak' we'll say,
To all our friends and relations
Who will come on this festival day.

I've helped mum make lots of samosas
And barfi – my favourite sweet.
First we'll all go to the mandir,
Then come back for our festival treat.

When it's evening we'll light up the divas,
They'll twinkle and shine long and bright.
We'll tell tales of how Ram fought Ravana,
It's Ram's victory we'll remember tonight.

Jill Bennett

Happy Diwali

A candle is painted
on our classroom window.
Candles are burning
in the autumn night.
Outside the west winds blow
but can't put out the candle for
the Festival of Light.

Nor our words, in yellow,
orange, red and white –
Happy Diwali!

Ann Bonner

Christmas travellers

The frost was hard,
the snowdrifts deep
when Shepherds left
their flock of sheep
and glimpsed the child
asleep, asleep.

A new star shone
on three Wise Men.
Each wore a cloak
and diadem.
From far they came
to Bethlehem.

Wes Magee

Christmas wishes

If I had three Christmas wishes
My first wish would be
For an end to hunger and poverty.

If I had three Christmas wishes
My second would be for
An end to violence, hatred and war.

If I had three Christmas wishes
My third wish would be
That we take proper care
of the land and the sea.

John Foster

Islands

Christmas Island must be magic,
winter every day –
snow for throwing,
ice for sliding,
gliding to school on a sleigh!

Easter Island must be great,
a dozen eggs a day –
look and lick,
be quick deciding –
hiding them's the safest way!

Birthday Island must be brilliant,
parties every day –
candle-blowing,
wish-inside-ing,
riding my new bike – hurray!

Sue Cowling

Happy Christmas

In Spain, there are no reindeer.
In France, no mistletoe.
In Russia, there's no roast pork.
No sleighs in Mexico.

In Panama, the weather's hot.
In Congo, there's no snow.
But Christmastime means Peace and Love
No matter where you go.

Ian Larmont

Chinese New Year

Snick, snack, clatter and clack!
Picketty, pocketty, pow!
Let's all wake the dragon up,
Make a mighty row!

Happiness and prosperity
Are yours the whole year through –
Let the dragon on his way
Take a gift from you.

Tick, tack! Firecrackers smack!
Old hundred-legs is here.
Wham and bang! and clash and clang!
Happy, happy New Year!

Dorothy Richards

Index of Poets

Index of First Lines

Index of Themes